Rapid Debt-Reduction Strategies

Financial Freedom Series,
Volume II

Rapid Debt-Reduction Strategies

Financial Freedom Series,
Volume II

By John Avanzini

HIS Publishing Company
Hurst, Texas

*Rapid Debt-Reduction Strategies —
Financial Freedom Series, Volume II*

ISBN 1-878605-01-1

First edition, 5,000 copies, 1990
Second edition, 30,000 copies, 1990
Third edition, 90,000 copies, 1990

Unless otherwise indicated, all Scripture quotations are
taken from the *King James Version* of the Bible.

Cover design and illustration by Bob Haddad.

Verses from *The Living Bible* are used by permission of
Tyndale House Publishers, Inc., Wheaton, Illinois
60189. All rights reserved.

HIS Publishing Company
P. O. Box 1096
Hurst, Texas 76053

This book is lovingly
dedicated to
Chris and Rona Avanzini,
who raised me in a home full of love,
and by their example,
instilled in me good moral standards
and a strong work ethic.
I could not have better parents if I had been allowed
to choose them myself from all the parents in the world.

Contents

Special Notice

The Information In This Book Is Given In Accordance With The Statement Written Below.

This book is intended to provide you with lay advice on ways and means of overcoming debt and is not intended as a substitute for **sound legal and accounting advice** from your attorney or financial advisor.

These are procedural suggestions, **not specific directions.** Before acting on any of these suggestions, you should thoroughly check what has been written to determine the proper course of action you should take. No two financial situations are exactly alike. **Always seek professional counsel before making changes in your financial matters.**

Anything you attempt to do toward the rapid reduction of any loan must be in agreement with that loan's legal document. The lender, as well as the borrower, has the right to reject any procedure that is not specified in the loan agreement.

The information in this book is, to the author's knowledge, conceptually correct. The mathematics used in the amortization schedules are based on standard mathematical formulas. The exact numbers may vary slightly from other amortization schedules due to the manner in which numbers are rounded. There may also be a difference due to the way the interest is calculated. (Some loans are figured on a 365-day year while others are figured on a 360-day year.)

Please remember that there are hundreds of possible combinations of interest, principal amounts and contractual agreements which may make it impossible to apply everything in this book to all loans. The examples herein are only given to illustrate the concepts explained. Even if they seem to fit your particular circumstances, your lending agreement and attorney's advice will supercede any suggestion made.

If your loan agreement contains anything that is not in accordance with federal, state, or local laws, neither this publication, its author, nor its owners will seek remedy for you or provide you with advice concerning relief. If your loan company will not allow you to operate any of the strategies in this book, neither this publication, its author, nor its owners will attempt to dissuade them or speak to them on your behalf. Your accountant or attorney should be contacted in such matters at your own expense.

Introduction

You Now Have A Plan

"For which of you, intending to build a tower, sitteth not down first, and counteth the cost. . . ."
Luke 14:28

If you do not have an **out-of-debt plan**, rest assured you are under the influence of someone else's **into-debt plan**. If you do not learn anything else from this book, I want you to realize that anytime money is involved, **nothing just happens by itself.** There is always a strategy at work — one that will either force money **into your hands** or force money **out of your hands.** If you are to be successful in the realm of finance, **you need** a well-formed plan to keep you out of debt's control.

No matter how bad your finances might be — no matter how hopeless things seem — rest in the knowledge **that you now have a plan available to you.** It is a plan that has successfully helped folks much like you to get out of debt. From this day on you no longer have to be a clay pigeon in the shooting gallery of debt. You are about to learn a special plan and a group of strategies which can make you debt free and give you financial independence.

Credit Comes Of Age

In the last thirty years, the credit industry has come into full maturity. No longer is it just a convenience made available to those who cannot pay cash. It is a full-grown,

15

multi-billion dollar industry which **sells its services** as a part of **every financial transaction** you enter. Apparently, multiplied billions of dollars are being spent annually by the credit industry to project the **illusion** that the easy-payment plan is helping the population into a better lifestyle. It is high time that we **wake up** and examine whether or not that is true.

No Holds Barred

Each and every day the unrelenting devourer called "interest" is eating a **bigger bite out of every dollar** being spent. It seems that every possible advantage available is being taken by the "easy-payment industry" **to keep you permanently in as much debt as you can possibly pay.** Make no mistake about it. **It is not a coincidence that you cannot seem to get out of debt**. It appears to be the result of a well-executed plan.

If your credit rating is good, new strategies are apparently being devised **to get you deeper into debt.** Once you are in to your limit, they seem to work to **keep you there for the rest of your life.** If you are to survive this relentless attack against your assets, you must **fight back** with a **master plan of your own.** I don't mean a plan that will just get you out of debt. I am speaking of a plan that **will get you out and keep you out.** It's time for you to declare all-out **war on debt!**

The master plan in this book **is not an experiment.** This plan has been proven time and again. It has worked in my life as well as in the lives of others. When my wife and I faithfully executed it, this plan rapidly took us from the depths of debt into **the completely debt-free lifestyle** we now enjoy.

Buried In Debt

When I say we were in debt, believe me, **we were buried in it.** Even the experts said our case was hopeless. The only advice anyone gave us about our financial situation **was to immediately file bankruptcy.**

As unbelievable as it seems today, **the master plan** in this book quickly brought us out of debt. Our payout took place so rapidly that some of **our most skeptical creditors** actually asked us to explain to them **how we were able to make such a rapid recovery** from such an overwhelming debt load.

Our Knowledge Was Limited

When we came out of debt the first time, we did not understand that it was possible to live without owing money on our automobile, home, or big-ticket items. I am ashamed of what I must now confess, but in the years that followed, we **drifted right back into the bondage of debt.** We accumulated loans on the television, appliances, second mortgages, credit cards, and so on. **It wasn't long until** we were once again **up to our eyeballs in debt!**

At this time, we realized that without a plan to **stay out of the grip of debt** we would continually **fall back into debt.**

The second time we approached our debt payoff, we made up our minds to become **totally debt free.** To accomplish this, we realized we would have to **change our basic mentality.** If we did not do so, we would have no way to **keep from being trapped by debt again.**

It's Not Wrong To Borrow

Please note that I do not believe in **never borrowing.** In a time of need, **a properly handled loan** can serve you well. However, there is **a very special philosophy** that must be applied to any loan which is made **if that loan is not to rule you!** I will be thoroughly explaining this philosophy to you in the last chapter of this book.

This Time The Mortgage Would Go

The second time we rapidly paid our way out of debt, we had some new artillery, for we had discovered some things about mortgages that I wonder if **the lenders wanted us to know.** Not only am I curious as to whether they wanted us to know, I would like to hear how they feel about my letting you know. We found that there were some **strategic ways of paying a mortgage** that automatically cut many years off the loan. Not only were years cut off, but in the process, we were able to **save thousands,**

even tens of thousands of dollars off the actual cash outlay that was called for in our thirty-year loan.

This Time Car Notes Would Also Go

We also learned a strategy which made it possible for us to purchase the very best of automobiles on a 90 to 120-day loan instead of paying for them over a five-year period. **Sometimes we are even able to pay cash on delivery.**

In this book, all these strategies are made available to you. As you read it, realize that some consultants are charging hundreds, and even thousands of dollars to help people in matters such as this. I believe that as you read, you will find **answers** to your own debt dilemma.

You Can Do It

Do not be afraid that you will not be able to do it. It is easier **when you know how.** Remember, it was someone else's "into-debt strategies" that brought you into your present financial mess. Now, **your own "out-of-debt strategy"** is available to help you rapidly get yourself out of that mess. **There is always help for those who try to help themselves.**

Section I

Getting Organized

Once you **get organized** and experience just how good that feels, you will wonder why it took you so long to get around to it.

It seems common among people who are deeply in debt to be disorganized. It seems the worse their debt situation becomes, the more disorganized they are. There is a deep sense of hopelessness that accompanies chronic debt problems. This hopelessness contributes to all kinds of disorder in their lives.

These first two chapters will be a real help to you. From them you will receive vital information which will help you more effectively start your out-of-debt strategy. They will also give you the personal satisfaction of feeling you are once again **taking control of your finances.**

Chapter One will help you better understand the extent of your debt problem. As you get organized, you will realize the **amount you actually owe.** This is usually a painful experience. But, if you notice, you will also be making a list of **things you own.** These are your assets. Some of them will become very valuable to you, for among them you will find some things which will actually help you get out of debt.

Chapter Two will deal with the things you will sell to help you pay off some of your bills. Many of these items will be things you impulsively purchased — items that are now out of sight and mind. This survey will bring them to the surface where they can be turned into much needed cash. Keep in mind that this will be very special cash, for it will be used to start your **war on debt**. It will become dynamite in your hands.

Please do not skip over the information in these two chapters. It is very important. All most people need to get started is the little bit of an edge this section can give them. The more thorough you are in these two chapters, the quicker you will be on the road to financial freedom.

Let's get started!

1

Know Where You Are

It is impossible to navigate an airplane to a predetermined destination unless **you know where you are**. It does not matter how advanced your navigational equipment might be. If you cannot determine **your present position,** it will be very difficult to reach **a desired destination.**

Make Two Lists

The very same principle is true when it comes to getting out of debt. Two points of reference are needed. **First,** you must know **exactly how much you owe.** **Second,** you must know **exactly how much you own.**

At the end of this chapter, you will find two sample lists. One is titled, **"How Much I Owe."** The other is titled, **"Things I Own."** Because of the limited page size in this book, it will be necessary for you to construct your own lists using these sample lists as models. Fill them out as completely and accurately as possible.

When you have completed them, they will help you more clearly understand your present financial position. With this information in hand, you can begin to more easily manage your finances in a way that will serve your best interests. The importance of these lists will become more evident as you proceed.

You Must Know What You Owe

Complete the "**How Much I Owe**" list first. I am sure **this will be the most painful part of the entire process.** It will take some real strength and dedication to your purpose to complete this form. You will probably want to kick yourself when you see some of the foolish things you have allowed the spirit of debt to influence you to do.

Don't Leave Anything Out

Every bill should be listed. **Each one is important.** Any debt you omit will make **your position weaker** and **your debt's position stronger.** List each bill, its due date, the interest rate, and the dollar amount of each payment. Be sure to accurately list the remaining balance. The number of payments left should be counted and listed for each item.

What Should Really Count

Don't be too rough on yourself. What should really count is not that you are in debt, but that **you are doing something about it.** Keep reminding yourself that what you are doing is **not a temporary, stop-gap measure.** It will lead to **a permanent solution.** As you look at the growing list of what you owe, you may think there is no use going any further. Please do not let that type of thinking stop you. If you do, this book cannot help you. **Take my word for it.** If you continue, you will be glad you did. No matter how painful it is, you must continue until all your debts are listed.

You Must Know What You Own

If you are like most people, you have accumulated many things over the years. When the list is completed, **it may well surprise you** to see how many things you actually own. When your possessions are scattered around the house, yard, and neighborhood, it is difficult to clearly understand just what you have.

As you make your list, be thorough. The more exact you are, **the more powerful your war on debt** will be.

Sample List

How Much I Owe

Bill Owed	Orig. Amt.	Int. Rate	Bal.	# Pmts. Remaining	Payoff Date

Footnote: Financial Freedom Series, Volume III, a debt-reduction workbook, contains these and many other ready-made forms. Available from HIS Publishing Company, Hurst, Texas 76053.

Sample List

<u>Things I Own</u>

(Check "Not" if item is not needed. Check "Need" if item is needed. Check "Want" if item is not needed, but wanted.)

Item	Cost	Loan	Not	Need	Want	Value	Sell

Footnote: Financial Freedom Series, Volume III, a debt-reduction workbook, contains these and other ready-made forms. Available from HIS Publishing Company, Hurst, Texas 76053.

2

Use It, Or Sell It

In the previous chapter, one of the lists you were asked to compile was **"Things I Own."** You were asked to indicate the present value of each item you listed. You also wrote down how much, if anything, you still owe.

You were asked to make a very important decision about each item. You had to decide whether or not you still needed it. Be assured, this was not just an incidental question. It is a very important part of your accelerated, out-of-debt strategy.

I Would Like To Keep It

You were also asked to indicate the items you do not need but **would like to keep.** These items should be clearly distinguished from the items **you do not want to keep.** With this information, you can now begin to intelligently build a list of **the things you will sell.** As you begin this list, you will quickly see why it was so important to fill in every blank on both lists.

Not Everything Can Be Sold

At the end of this chapter you will find a model form listing "Things I Must Sell," which should be reconstructed on a larger sheet of paper. As you list these things, pay close attention to the items on which you still owe money. It is very important that you thoroughly read your loan agreement. Before you try to sell anything which still has money owing, you must be sure there is no restriction which forbids selling it before it is paid off. There may also be other peculiarities that call for a different approach. If you have any question about whether something can be sold or not, ask the lender and check with your attorney.

Be Rational

Don't get caught up in the spirit of selling and **mistakenly part with something you really need.** You must be even more careful when considering the items listed as things you don't need but would like to keep. Your good judgement must be used to be sure you **do not mistakenly sell something which might end up being one of your primary forms of enjoyment during the time you are getting out of debt.**

For instance, a bicycle you no longer use may be a lot of fun when **credit card financed entertainment** is no longer available. You may not be using a certain piece of exercise equipment now. However, it might be much more useful to you in the months ahead. It might just help you let off some steam.

A Simple Test

A simple test for determining if an item should be kept or sold is listed below:

1. Do I really want to sell the item?
2. Will I enjoy having the item more than I will enjoy paying off the portion of debt that its sale would accomplish?
3. Will the item become of greater value to me during the months ahead?

With this simple, three-step test, you should be able to easily make quality decisions as to what you should keep and what you should sell.

Now, begin to make the list of things you will sell. Remember, the money you raise from their sale will be used to make a major paydown of the debts you now owe. See Section VII for some suggestions which might help you with their sale.

Sample List

<u>Things I Must Sell</u>

Item	Orignal Cost	Selling Price

Footnote: Financial Freedom Series, Volume III, a debt-reduction workbook, contains these and many other ready-made forms. Available from HIS Publishing Company, Hurst, Texas 76053.

Section II

The Master Plan Strategy

It is now time to explain **"the master plan."** This is the miracle plan that my wife and I discovered during the late 1960's. This was a time in our lives when it seemed absolutely impossible for us to **ever get all our bills paid.**

We Owed Big Money

We owed huge amounts of money. Our debt included **a number of major credit cards,** every one of them **charged to its limit.** At least three cards had balances over $10,000. Besides the credit card debt, we owed **several signature loans to banks.**

Our **numerous gasoline credit cards** had long since been canceled, leaving enormous unpaid balances. Every one of our **department store cards** was at its maximum allowable limit. Payments on several **loans from individuals** were in delinquency. **Our previous year's income tax** payment was six months overdue. Both of our new **automobiles had been repossessed.** Our three **homes were taken from us through foreclosure.**

It Was Worse Than Bad

To say our situation was bad would be a **great understatement. It was impossible!** We were no longer able to even maintain a home for our five children. **We lived with my father and mother.**

Anyone who was an adult during the late sixties will quickly tell you that by today's inflated prices, our debt would have been **at least four times greater.**

It Seemed Bankruptcy Was Our Only Hope

With this **mountain of debt towering over us,** we were faced with the heaviest of decisions. **Should we take bankruptcy,** as most people were advising, or **should we somehow try to dig our way out** of this avalanche of **unpaid bills?** If we chose to pay our way out, **it would take years.** All of our plans would have to be put on hold! We would be faced with the dismal task of doing nothing more than **paying bills for the next six to ten years.**

I must admit that **bankruptcy seemed to be our only hope.** We had lived under financial pressure for so long that **our thinking process had become flawed.** We had come to the point that we could **no longer see ourselves ever being debt free again.** Neither could we bear the thought of facing the mountain of bills which were **systematically destroying our joy as well as our marriage.** We were living exactly as the Scripture says:

"... the borrower is servant to the lender."
Proverbs 22:7

As I look back, I am so thankful for the revelation of **the master plan.** It was so wonderful to get control of our debts and begin to pay them off that I made up my mind one day I would help others become debt free. Now that I am able to do so, **I present to you the master plan.** I hope it brings you the joy it gave to my loved ones and me.

3

The Master Plan

I am the type of person who has always been intrigued by mathematics. I can remember times when I would sit up all night with a calculator. I would figure how much money I could save if I put only $100 a month in the bank. I would work out elaborate interest tables showing me year by year and month by month how quickly my money could grow. I would calculate these savings plans up to age sixty-five.

With my calculator, I even figured how to more rapidly pay off my mortgage. I discovered a few **special ways** of making my payments that would **drastically reduce my overall interest costs.** But, even though I had the know-how to save, **for some reason I never did.** I just figured these wonderful things out on paper and never applied them to my finances.

I Was Addicted To Credit

I finally realized my problem. I was **hopelessly addicted to credit buying.** I was being held captive under the power of debt. **It was not until I broke that compulsion** that I was able to successfully put these plans to work.

On the eve of making our decision to take bankruptcy, I said to my wife, "Pat, let me spend **one last night with these bills** and see if there isn't some way to get them paid off."

The Plan Is Revealed

That night I made many calculations. I looked at my bills from every conceivable angle. **Then, all of a sudden, "the master plan"** was revealed to me. It came as a **complete surprise.** When I saw it, I was amazed that I had never thought of it before. Not only had I never thought of it, I had never even heard of it before. The plan is **so simple,** yet **so powerful.** When I showed it to my wife the next morning, **she immediately confirmed that it would work.**

The Plan

As I now begin to explain what was **revealed** to me that night, please **pay very close attention.** At first it may seem **too simple to work on such a complex problem** as the one you face. However, if you will give it **an honest try,** I am confident it will bring you **out of debt in quick order.**

Footnote: *See <u>War On Debt, Breaking the Power of Debt</u>, Financial Freedom Series, Volume I, for information on breaking the power of credit addiction. Available from HIS Publishing Company, Hurst, Texas 76053.*

If you notice, I call this **"the master plan."** In the following chapter, you will see that no other name would fit. Just open your mind, follow with me, and see if this plan makes sense to you.

One Big Bill

The first step that must be made in taking dominion over your bills is to stop looking at them as if they are **many bills.** From this day forward, you **must** look at them as if they are combined into **one, giant bill.**

One Big Payment

Now, don't let the thought of one big bill throw you. **It is not as bad as it sounds.** Granted, you will now be dealing with your bills as if they are one **giant bill**, but you will also do the same with your many payments. From this day forward you must consider that you have one **great, big payment** to make on that big bill. This giant payment will consist of the total amount of all your present payments added together.

Now here is the power behind this. While your **big bill will become less** each time one of the smaller bills is paid off, your **big payment will stay the same** until the last bill is paid in full. Do you see how special this makes your one, big payment? **It will become more powerful** each time one of your bills is paid off, for it will then be able to do more toward paying off your remaining debt.

Step by step, with the payoff of each bill, your payment will be able to eliminate more and more of your debt. At some point in time, it may even **seem that your payment has doubled,** or even **tripled** in value. I can hear you ask the question, **"How can this be?"**

For illustration purposes, let's say you owe a total of $20,000 on your combined bills. If you continue to pay them at the minimum allowable payments each month, it is obvious that you will spend many years making payments on them before they are all paid.

Let's say your payments total up to $1,400 per month. Suppose this amount is made up of between twelve and twenty bills ranging in payments from $7.50 per month to a car note of $220 per month. If you have listed these bills on your "How Much I Owe" list (see Chapter 2), you will see that none of them pay off on the same date. You may still owe sixty payments on one, fourteen payments on another, and maybe only three more payments on yet another one.

Now, get this firmly in your mind. Your new, giant payment of $1,400 **must be faithfully made each and every month until every last bill is paid in full.** Yes, you read right. When a bill is paid off, the monthly payment <u>does not</u>, I repeat, <u>does not go down.</u>

Targeted For Destruction

Now, focus on the bill which will be paid in full in only three months. Suppose its payment is $80. Remember!

When this bill is paid, **you are not going to have an extra $80 to spend.** Instead you are going to have $80 **extra to apply to the next bill** you target for destruction.

Now, **pay close attention.** The next bill scheduled for destruction will not necessarily be the bill with the least number of payments remaining. You must **target the bill with the highest monthly payment** that the extra $80 per month will pay off the **fastest.**

Think Before You Act

Clear thinking is important at this point. Suppose you have a bill that will be paid off in three months if you apply your extra $80 to it. If that bill has a payment of $75 per month, **it may not be the best one to pay off next.** It would be better to use your extra $80 on a bill with **a higher monthly payment,** even though it may take **a little longer to pay.**

For example, if you have a bill with a $125 monthly payment which is close to being paid off, add your extra $80 to that bill each month. **Even if it takes an extra month or two** to pay it off, it is worth waiting in order to have an additional $125 every month to apply toward other bills.

The reason behind this is easy to understand. If you pay off the $75 monthly bill, you will only have $155 extra each month ($80 + $75) to apply against the next bill. However, if you pay off the $125 a month bill, you will have

$205 extra each month ($80 + $125) to use toward your next bill.

Pay Off The Car In Only A Few Months

During the final months of your master plan payoff, you will be paying bills off in one month that would have taken as long as a year at the minimum payments. There will also be a day when you can apply the entire $1,400 per month to your automobile loan (the monthly payment of all bills added to the car note). This will allow you to pay off the car in only a few months instead of the remaining three or four years which the regular payment would have taken.

Pay Off The House Next

When the entire $1,400 is available, why not take four or five hundred dollars for your regular monthly spending; then apply the extra $900 to $1,000 each month to your home mortgage. Why, in just a few more years, you will **really be debt free.** (See Section III for rapid mortgage payment strategies.)

4

Introducing The Author Of The Master Plan

Sleep usually comes naturally when you are mentally or physically exhausted. While this is true in most cases, it is not true when **uncontrolled debt** is involved. The unrelenting pursuit of the creditors can bring an intense weariness upon you. Joy leaves, and **of all things, sleeplessness sets in.** At these times it may seem that just one good night's sleep would make everything better, but **try as you might, sleep eludes you.**

When All Natural Solutions Fail

When natural solutions stop working, it is time to look beyond the natural. That is exactly what my wife and I did when our debt dilemma reached its most intense stage. We had followed the rules of the credit industry, but suddenly they had no acceptable answers for our situation. Debt consolidation was out of the question, for we owed too much. Our debt had been restructured several times, and no more extensions were available. When we had tried every possible form of relief the system afforded, the only solution the natural realm held out to us was bankruptcy.

Bankruptcy Was Not An Answer

Bankruptcy was not going to solve anything for us because with it would come a stigma which would make it extremely difficult, if not impossible, for us to continue our vocation. As ministers, bankruptcy would leave an ugly mark on our record. Please understand that I am not saying ministries cannot suffer bankruptcy and still continue successfully. I am merely saying that **in our case,** it would have made things more difficult.

We Needed Something Beyond The Natural

To make it plain and simple, **we needed a miracle** — something the best of the natural realm could not produce. That last night I spent trying to find an alternative to bankruptcy was a very special night. For a solution, I reached beyond the natural into the **supernatural. I reached out to God!**

A Terrifying Thought To Some

For some reason, the very mention of God seems to terrify some people and "turn off" others. However, under certain circumstances, the thought of reaching out to God is not only acceptable to them, but even comforting. The point where reaching out to Him **begins to make sense to most people** is when they come face to face with an event which goes beyond the realm of natural solutions. If your debt problems have brought you to this point, what I am about to share with you will not seem so strange. The pressures debt can cause find their origin beyond the realm of natural phenomenon.

There Is A Link

It is sometimes difficult for the technological mindset of our day to embrace the idea of God. However, there is a God-link which makes the act of reaching out to Him for help easier than you might think. The link I am speaking of is not a point of contact produced by our technological age. It is a point of contact provided by God Himself. I am speaking of the only **unfailing link — the man, Christ Jesus**. I am so thankful that I had previously accepted Him as my Savior. Because of this I could confidently reach out and touch God, through Jesus, in my hour of need.

It Was Revealed

On the eve of bankruptcy, **the master plan** was revealed to me — not by some metaphysical experience, but by my simple faith in Christ and His ability to save me from all my troubles. As I prayed to God for a miracle to get us out of pending disaster, He heard and responded by giving me a plan which would bring me into a debt-free lifestyle.

If you are at a point in your life where natural remedies no longer hold out any hope — if you feel as if the system has given up on you — my friend, **what you need is a miracle** from the only One who can perform it — God

Himself! He has provided a very special God-link for you — Jesus. Jesus is the Son of God, and He has already proven His love for you by dying on the cross of Calvary for your sins. If you think for a moment that God doesn't care about your problems, think again. The Bible says:

> **"He that spared not his own Son, but delivered him up for us all, how shall he not with him also freely give us all things?"**
> **Romans 8:32**

I do not care how bad things are, God has an answer. God Himself said to Abraham of old that He is able to do anything.

> **"Is any thing too hard for the Lord? . . ."**
> **Genesis 18:14**

Your Answer Is On The Way

Even as the answer I needed was given to me the night I prayed, **your answer from God is already on the way.** If you know Jesus Christ as your personal Savior, call out to Him for help. **He will answer!** If your relationship with Him has been temporarily interrupted by sin, **repent and return to Him this moment!** If you have never accepted Him as Savior, **do so now!** The Bible tells us:

> **"For whosoever shall call upon the name of the Lord shall be saved."**
> **Romans 10:13**

It is so simple to call upon Him. Just bow your head and ask Him to come into your heart. There is a prayer called **"the prayer of salvation."** It is simple:

"Dear Lord Jesus, please forgive me of my sins. Come into my heart, and save me."

Sincerely speak these words from your heart, and make Jesus your Lord and Savior. Will it work? The Bible says it will.

"For whosoever shall call upon the name of the Lord shall be saved."
Romans 10:13

Be Specific

Now that you know Jesus as your own personal Savior, ask Him for the specific help you need. Go ahead and **boldly ask Him for your miracle** — that special intervention from the supernatural realm into the natural. Your God can provide the solution now that you have the God-link, Jesus the Christ. Think of it! The Son of the Living God is now living in you.

Drop Me A Line

You have now been introduced to the author of **the master plan.** If you have accepted Him as a result of this book, drop me a line and tell me about it. My address can be found at the back of this book.

Thank you for your attention to this chapter, for this is **the master strategy of all strategies, salvation by Jesus Christ.**

If you have not yet read Volume I of this series, I suggest that you do so at your earliest convenience, **for only then will the information in this book be complete.**

Footnote: See <u>War</u> <u>On</u> <u>Debt</u>, <u>Breaking</u> <u>the</u> <u>Power</u> <u>of</u> <u>Debt</u>, Financial Freedom Series, Volume I which gives a complete spiritual plan to break debt's hold on you and bring you into the liberty of the debt-free life. Available from HIS Publishing Company, Hurst, Texas 75063.

Section III

Ten Powerful Mortgage Payment Strategies

It would take most people the greater part of their lives to save enough money to pay cash for a home. When this is considered in conjunction with the ever-increasing cost of houses, it becomes evident that home ownership must be accomplished as soon as possible, **even if you must borrow to do it.**

You Can Have A Debt-Free Home

The person who desires to buy a home, but must use monthly payments, can now safely do so. The time-payment purchase of a home no longer has to take thirty years. I say this because many borrowing **secrets** have been discovered. With these discoveries, **effective strategies have been calculated** giving the informed borrower the advantage. If your mortgage is approached with the strict resolve **of paying it off as soon as possible,** many years and thousands of dollars can be saved off the traditional thirty-year home loan. The key ingredient in **taking control of your mortgage** is an unswerving determination that you will, **under no circumstances**, take thirty years to pay it off. To do this **you must employ one or more effective strategies.**

49

The Mathematical Advantage

There are **powerful mathematical facts** that you, the home buyer, can now know about mortgages. You must make additional paydowns for any rapid debt-reduction strategy to work. While there is no strategy which will lower the principal amount you borrow, there are a number of ways to **drastically lower the interest costs** which the lender will be legally entitled to collect from you.

The following strategies are **mathematically sound** methods which can greatly reduce the **expense, as well as the time** it takes to pay off your home loan. Each strategy is **conceptually correct.** However, it is your responsibility to get the lending institution which holds your loan to agree to any modifications made to your present loan agreement. Remember, your mortgage holder is not obligated to do anything not expressly stated in the loan agreement you signed.

Do not become discouraged at this statement. If your mortgage does not expressly forbid prepayment, ninety percent of the obstacles are already out of the way. I am sure you can make some, if not all of the following rapid payoff strategies work for you.

If The Bank Says "No"

If your banker rejects your rapid payoff plan, **don't give up.** "It's not over until it's over." There still may be something you can do. First, find out if your present loan has any form of prepayment restriction. This may be wording that says **you cannot pay off the principal in advance,** or it may state that **a payoff penalty will be charged if you do so.** In many states it is now illegal for a lender to refuse a home owner the right to prepay his mortgage.

Be Courteous

Courteously ask your loan officer if you can begin prepaying the principal due on your mortgage. Give him an opportunity to agree. However, if he says "no," thank him and leave. **But do not give up hope.** Try one more thing before contacting your state's banking authority for help. Just as if nothing had ever been said, go right ahead with your plan for a rapid payoff. Mail in your payment as you always do, enclosing the regular monthly amount, plus any additional amount you wish to prepay on the principal balance.

Write One Check

When you make your payments, **do not write two checks.** Add any extra amount you wish to pay on your loan to the check you would normally send. It has been reported that these payments are almost never refused by the bookkeeping departments of lending institutions. They usually just apply the extra payment to the principal without any further discussion.

Keep Good Records

Warning! Once you begin a rapid debt-reduction strategy, always check that your entire regular payment **and all of your prepayments** have been accepted and **properly credited to your account.** It is absolutely necessary that you keep a file of the canceled checks for all payments you make. Always attach the receipt to the check. Begin your file on the date you first make a prepayment until your loan is paid in full. **Always insist** that the bookkeeping department of your lending institution provide you a correct balance with each month's receipt. Check that this new balance includes a deduction of your prepayment for that month.

Rapid mortgage reduction will only take place **if every payment you make is properly recorded.** Your canceled check, coupled with your lender's monthly statement **showing your paydown** should be sufficient evidence of payment. Do not make the mistake of keeping only a **copy** of each check you write. You must also **keep the original check,** for the lender's endorsement **will appear on the back** of each one. This is proof that they accepted your payment.

Footnote: All mortgage payment strategies should be operated with a personalized amortization schedule in your possession. You will find details in Chapter 15 of how to obtain a tailor-made amortization schedule of your mortgage.

5

The First-Day Payment Strategy

Let's begin this section with one of the most powerful prepayment strategies in existence. It is an amazing way to quickly reduce the balance on your mortgage while also greatly reducing the time it takes to pay it off.

To get the greatest benefit from this strategy you must make the first payment on your loan **the day it is activated.** By this I mean the first payment must be made **on the day the lender begins to charge interest** on the money you are borrowing. If this is done, an unbelievable number of months **will automatically be deducted** from the full term of your loan. In some cases your thirty-year mortgage can be shortened by more than **four years.** Think of it. All of that savings is yours by simply making one payment in advance. Keep in mind that the exact amount of savings **fluctuates with the interest rate** and term that apply to each mortgage.

An Example

In the case of a $100,000 mortgage with an interest rate of 14.5%, you will deduct four years and six months from the term of the loan by this simple strategy. This thirty-year mortgage will be automatically reduced to twenty-five and a half years. You can actually save four and a half years of payments (54 months) **by making only one payment at the right time.** This will also cause a great interest savings to occur. In the case of a $100,000 mortgage at this rate, the interest savings will be $64,900.48.

How It Works

This strategy works so well because during the first years of your mortgage only a small part of each monthly payment is applied to lowering your principal balance. With the $100,000 mortgage example, if the first payment is made on the due date, only $16.23 of the $1,224.56 payment is used to pay off the balance. This means that **a whopping $1,208.33 of that first payment goes toward interest.** However, if the first payment of $1,224.56 is made before any interest is charged, the full amount of the payment goes toward paying off your $100,000 balance.

Amazing

Now see some amazing facts about the savings this strategy makes on the above mentioned mortgage. You would have to pay the $1,224.56 payment for **a full twelve years and nine months** before even $100 of each payment would be applied to your mortgage balance. Keep this in mind. If you pay according to the thirty-year plan, the major portion of every payment will be paying interest **for almost the entire life of your mortgage.** Your only hope of saving money comes from the amount of interest you can eliminate by prepaying the principal.

Not Necessarily A First-Payment Strategy

This strategy can be applied at any time during the life of your mortgage. However, it will never accomplish more drastic results than it does with the first payment. Whenever it is applied, it will bring big results.

The More, The Merrier

I have projected this plan in several different ways at the end of this chapter. By these comparisons you will be able to see what a substantial difference is made in a loan **by making two, three, four, or five payments** on the day the loan is made. With each additional payment you are able to make on the first day, your mortgage is even more drastically shortened.

Give A Really Big Gift To Your Children

This strategy is a great way for parents to give their children a really big annuity. Using a $100,000 mortgage at 14.5% interest, if you make only **five payments** for your children on the day they borrow the money, your gift will cost $6,122.80. However, you will actually be giving them **a gift worth $168,947.76. This is the amount of interest they will never have to pay on that loan.** And that's not all. You will shorten their thirty-year mortgage by **eleven years and nine months.** That means their thirty-year mortgage will automatically become a **nineteen-year, three-month mortgage.** Just think of how nice this gift would be for a loved one!

When you begin to use this first-day payment strategy, **you take control of your mortgage.** Keep in mind that after you have applied this strategy, **you can still apply one or more of the other strategies** from the following chapters to pay off your loan even more rapidly.

Say "No" To The Loan Officer

It has been brought to my attention that when some people try to execute this strategy, **they meet resistance.** The loan officer tries to tell them they cannot pay any payments on the day they borrow the money. After some insistence, some loan officers reluctantly suggest that the borrower just borrow a smaller amount. For instance, if the loan is $100,000 and the payment is $1,224.56, they suggest making the mortgage $98,776. ($100,000.00 – 1,224 = $98,776.)

Don't be fooled. This is not a rapid debt-reduction strategy. The loan of $98,776 will still take **thirty years to pay.** It will save you less than $100 a month from your payment. Remember, you must have a **reduction of years and interest cost** from your loan to have a **true rapid-reduction strategy.** To borrow $1,224 less only saves you $1,224 in principal. To pay down a $100,000 loan on day one with a $1,224.56 prepayment saves you four and a half years of payments (54 payments) and $64,900.48 in interest. **Don't be rude, but just say "no"** if the loan officer wants to get you off course.

While this strategy saves more on a loan under ten years of age, it will save money on any loan to which it is applied. The only way to completely understand the savings this strategy will make on your loan is to have an accurate amortization schedule showing the calculations applied to your particular mortgage. See Chapter 15 for information on how to obtain your personalized amortization schedule with this strategy applied.

Support Information
The First-Day Payment Strategy
15.5% Interest

Loan Amount	$100,000.00
Term	30 Years
Payment	$1,304.52

Pmt. No.	Pmt. Amt.	Mos. Saved	Yrs. Saved	Int. Saved	Yrs. to Payoff
1	$1,304.52	65	6yrs.6mo.	$83,497.31	23yrs.6mo.
2	2,609.04	100	8yrs.4mo.	127,856.23	21yrs.8mo.
3	3,913.56	124	10yrs.3mo.	157,869.53	19yrs.9mo.
4	5,218.08	143	11yrs.11mo.	181,306.26	18yrs.1mo.
5	6,522.60	157	13yrs.	198,342.37	17yrs.

This illustration shows what will happen when 1 through 5 payments are made before any interest is due. This strategy also works on existing mortgages.

Support Information
The First-Day Payment Strategy
15.5% Interest Continued

Pmt. Amt.	Prin.	Pmt. No.	Int.	Bal.	Total Int.
$1,304.52	12.85	1	$1,291.67	$99,987.15	
1,304.52	13.02	2	1,291.50	99,974.13	$2,583.17
1,304.52	13.18	3	1,291.33	99,960.95	3,874.50

Payments 4 through 63 omitted to conserve space.

$1,304.52	28.84	64	1,275.67	98,732.93	82,222.01

One First-Day Payment

1,304.52	29.22	65	1,275.30	98,703.71	83,497.31
1,304.52	29.59	66	1,274.92	98,674.12	84,772.23

Payments 67 through 98 omitted to conserve space.

1,304.52	45.20	99	1,259.32	97,450.32	126,597.50

Two First-Day Payments

1,304.52	45.78	100	1,258.73	97,404.54	127,856.23
1,304.52	46.37	101	1,258.14	97,358.17	129,114.37

Payments 102 through 122 omitted to conserve space.

1,304.52	61.50	123	1,243.01	96,171.74	156,627.32

Three First-Day Payments

1,304.52	62.30	124	1,242.22	96,109.44	157,869.53
1,304.52	63.10	125	1,241.41	96,046.33	159,110.95

Payments 126 through 141 omitted to conserve space.

1,304.52	78.49	142	1,226.03	94,839.85	180,081.25

Four First-Day Payments

1,304.52	79.50	143	1,225.01	94,760.34	181,306.26
1,304.52	80.53	144	1,223.99	94,679.81	182,530.25

Payments 145 through 155 omitted to conserve space.

1,304.52	93.94	156	1,210.58	93,628.36	197,133.00

Five First-Day Payments

1,304.52	95.15	157	1,209.37	93,533.21	198,342.37
1,304.52	96.38	158	1,208.14	93,436.83	199,550.50

This illustration shows the effect of 1 through 5 first-day payments on a standard amortization schedule. The boxed number is how many payments are eliminated by making the first-day payment. The underlined number is the balance after making the first-day payment. The circled number is the interest saved.

Support Information
The First-Day Payment Strategy
15% Interest Rate

Loan Amount		$100,000.00
Term		30 Years
Payment		$1,264.44

Pmt. No.	Pmt. Amt.	Mos. Saved	Yrs. Saved	Int. Saved	Yrs. to Payoff
1	$1,264.44	60	5yrs.	$74,587.27	25yrs.
2	2,528.88	93	7yrs.9mo.	115,080.08	22yrs.3mo.
3	3,793.32	117	9yrs.9mo.	144,152.40	20yrs.3mo.
4	5,057.76	135	11yrs.3mo.	165,673.77	18yrs.9mo.
5	6,322.20	150	12yrs.6mo.	183,374.24	17yrs.6mo.

This illustration shows what will happen when 1 through 5 payments are made before any interest is due. This strategy also works on existing mortgages.

Support Information
The First-Day Payment Strategy
15% Interest Continued

Pmt. Amt.	Prin.	Pmt. No.	Int.	Bal.	Total Int.
$1,264.44	14.44	1	1,250.00	$99,985.56	
1,264.44	14.62	2	1,249.82	99,970.93	$2,499.82
1,264.44	14.81	3	1,249.64	99,956.12	3,749.46
Payments 4 through 58 omitted to conserve space.					
1,264.44	29.69	59	1,234.75	98,750.69	73,352.89
One First-Day Payment					
1,264.44	30.06	60	1,234.38	98,720.63	74,587.27
1,264.44	30.44	61	1,234.01	98,690.19	75,821.28
Payments 62 through 91 omitted to conserves space.					
1,264.44	44.73	92	1,219.71	97,532.08	113,860.93
Two First-Day Payments					
1,264.44	45.29	93	1,219.15	97,486.79	115,080.08
1,264.44	45.86	94	1,218.58	97,440.93	116,298.67
Payments 95 through 115 omitted to conserve space.					
1,264.44	60.27	116	1,204.17	96,273.48	142,948.98
Three First-Day Payments					
1,264.44	61.03	117	1,203.42	96,212.45	144,152.40
1,264.44	61.79	118	1,202.66	96,150.66	145,355.06
Payments 119 through 133 omitted to conserve space.					
1,264.44	75.38	134	1,189.07	95,050.15	164,485.64
Four First Day Payments					
1,264.44	76.32	135	1,188.13	94,973.83	165,673.77
1,264.44	77.27	136	1,187.17	94,896.56	166,860.94
Payment 137 through 148 omitted to conserve space.					
1,264.44	90.81	149	1,173.63	93,799.59	182,201.75
Five First-Day Payments					
1,264.44	91.95	150	1,172.49	93,707.64	183,374.24
1,264.44	93.10	151	1,171.35	93,614.54	184,545.59

This illustration shows the effect of 1 through 5 first-day payments on a standard amortization schedule. The boxed number is how many payments are eliminated by making the first-day payment. The underlined number is the balance after making the first-day payment. The circled number is the interest saved.

Support Information
The First-Day Payment Strategy
14.5% Interest Rate

Loan Amount		$100,000.00
Term		30 Years
Payment		$1,224.56

Pmt. No.	Pmt. Amt.	Mos. Saved	Yrs. Saved	Int. Saved	Yrs. to Payoff
1	$1,224.56	54	4yrs.6mo.	$64,900.48	25yrs.6mo.
2	2,449.12	87	7yrs.3mo.	104,061.69	22yrs.9mo.
3	3,673.68	110	9yrs.2mo.	131,011.91	20yrs.10mo.
4	4,898.24	128	10yrs.9mo.	151,839.51	19yrs.3mo.
5	6,122.80	143	11yrs.11mo.	168,974.76	18yrs.1mo.

This illustration shows what will happen when 1 through 5 payments are made before any interest is due. This strategy also works on existing mortgages.

Support Information
The First-Day Payment Strategy
14.5% Interest Continued

Pmt. Amt.	Prin.	Pmt. No.	Int.	Bal.	Total Int.
$1,224.56	16.22	1	$1,208.33	$99,983.78	
1,224.56	16.42	2	1,208.14	99,967.36	$2,416.47
1,224.56	16.62	3	1,207.94	99,950.74	3,624.41
Payments 4 through 52 omitted to conserve space.					
1,224.56	30.29	53	1,194.26	98,805.12	63,706.58
One First-Day Payment					
1,224.56	30.66	54	1,193.90	98,774.46	64,900.48
1,224.56	31.03	55	1,193.52	98,743.43	66,094.00
Payments 56 through 85 omitted to conserve space.					
1,224.56	45.03	86	1,179.53	97,570.90	102,882.70
Two First-Day Payments					
1,224.56	45.57	87	1,178.98	97,525.32	104,061.69
1,224.56	46.12	88	1,178.43	97,479.20	105,240.12
Payments 89 through 108 omitted to conserve space.					
1,224.56	59.36	109	1,165.20	96,370.83	129,847.43
Three First-Day Payments					
1,224.56	60.08	110	1,164.48	96,310.76	131,011.91
1,224.56	60.80	111	1,163.75	96,249.96	132,175.66
Payments 112 through 126 omitted to conserve space.					
1,224.56	73.68	127	1,150.87	95,170.92	150,689.53
Four First-Day Payments					
1,224.56	74.57	128	1,149.98	95,096.35	151,839.51
1,224.56	75.48	129	1,149.08	95,020.88	152,988.59
Payments 130 through 141 omitted to conserve space.					
1,224.56	88.23	142	1,136.33	93,952.56	167,839.50
Five First-Day Payments					
1,224.56	89.30	143	1,135.26	93,863.27	168,974.76
1,224.56	90.37	144	1,134.18	93,772.89	170,108.94

This illustration shows the effect of 1 through 5 first-day payments on a standard amortization schedule. The boxed number is how many payments are eliminated by making the first-day payment. The underlined number is the balance after making the first-day payment. The circled number is the interest saved.

Support Information
The First-Day Payment Strategy
14% Interest Rate

Loan Amount		$100,000.00
Term		30 Years
Payment		$1,184.87

Pmt. No.	Pmt. Amt.	Mos. Saved	Yrs. Saved	Int. Saved	Yrs. to Payoff
1	$1,184.87	49	4yrs.1mo.	$56,864.41	25yrs.11mo.
2	2,369.74	80	6yrs.11mo.	92,403.41	23yrs.1mo.
3	3,554.61	102	8yrs.6mo.	117,323.29	21yrs.6mo.
4	4,739.48	120	10yrs.	137,468.24	20yrs.
5	5,924.35	135	11yrs.3mo.	154,048.47	18yrs.9mo.

This illustration shows what will happen when 1 through 5 payments are made before any interest is due. This strategy also works on existing mortgages.

Support Information
The First-Day Payment Strategy
14% Interest Continued

Pmt. Amt.	Prin.	Pmt. No.	Int.	Bal.	Total Int.
$1,184.87	18.21	1	1,166.67	$99,981.79	
1,184.87	18.42	2	1,166.45	99,963.38	$2,333.12
1,184.87	18.63	3	1,166.24	99,944.75	3,499.36
Payments 4 through 47 omitted to conserve space.					
1,184.87	31.40	48	1,153.47	98,837.46	55,711.31
One First-Day Payment					
1,184.87	31.77	49	1,153.10	<u>98,805.70</u>	56,864.41
1,184.87	32.14	50	1,152.73	98,773.56	58,017.15
Payments 51 through 78 omitted to conserve space.					
1,184.87	44.99	79	1,139.88	97,659.19	91,264.05
Two First-Day Payments					
1,184.87	45.51	80	1,139.36	<u>97,613.67</u>	92,403.41
1,184.87	46.05	81	1,138.83	97,567.63	93,542.24
Payments 82 through 100 omitted to conserve space.					
1,184.87	58.07	101	1,126.80	96,525.11	116,197.16
Three First-Day Payments					
1,184.87	58.75	102	1,126.13	<u>96,466.37</u>	117,323.29
1,184.87	59.43	103	1,125.44	96,406.94	118,448.73
Payments 104 through 118 omitted to conserve space.					
1,184.87	71.55	119	1,113.32	95,356.01	136,355.75
Four First-Day Payments					
1,184.87	72.38	120	1,112.49	<u>95,283.63</u>	137,468.24
1,184.87	73.23	121	1,111.64	95,210.40	138,579.88
Payments 122 through 133 omitted to conserve space.					
1,184.87	85.15	134	1,099.72	94,176.92	152,949.74
Five First-Day Payments					
1,184.87	86.14	135	1,098.73	<u>94,090.78</u>	154,048.47
1,184.87	87.15	136	1,097.73	94,003.64	155,146.20

This illustration shows the effect of 1 through 5 first-day payments on a standard amortization schedule. The boxed number is how many payments are eliminated by making the first-day payment. The underlined number is the balance after making the first-day payment. The circled number is the interest saved.

Support Information
The First-Day Payment Strategy
13.5% Interest Rate

Loan Amount		$100,000.00
Term		30 Years
Payment		$1,145.41

Pmt. No.	Pmt. Amt.	Mos. Saved	Yrs. Saved	Int. Saved	Yrs. to Payoff
1	$1,145.41	44	3yrs.6mo.	$49,244.22	26yrs.6mo.
2	2,290.82	73	6yrs.1mo.	81,323.59	23yrs.11mo.
3	3,436.23	95	7yrs.11mo.	105,376.90	22yrs.11mo.
4	4,581.64	113	9yrs.5mo.	124,822.80	20yrs.7mo.
5	5,727.05	127	10yrs.7mo.	139,769.50	19yrs.5mo.

This illustration shows what will happen when 1 through 5 payments are made before any interest is due. This strategy also works on existing mortgages.

Support Information
The First-Day Payment Strategy
13.5% Interest Continued

Pmt. Amt.	Prin.	Pmt. No.	Int.	Bal.	Total Int.
$1,145.41	20.41	1	1,125.00	$99,979.59	
1,145.41	20.64	2	1,124.77	99,958.95	$2,249.77
1,145.41	20.87	3	1,124.54	99,938.07	3,374.31
Payments 4 through 42 omitted to conserve space.					
1,145.41	32.65	43	1,112.76	98,879.11	48,131.83
One First-Day Payment					
1,145.41	33.02	44	1,112.39	98,846.08	49,244.22
1,145.41	33.39	45	1,112.02	98,812.69	50,356.24
Payments 46 through 71 omitted to conserve space.					
1,145.41	45.17	72	1,100.24	97,754.18	80,223.86
Two First-Day Payments					
1,145.41	45.68	73	1,099.73	97,708.50	81,323.59
1,145.41	46.19	74	1,099.22	97,662.31	82,422.81
Payments 75 through 93 omitted to conserve space.					
1,145.41	57.77	94	1,087.64	96,621.17	104,289.91
Three First-Day Payments					
1,145.41	58.42	95	1,086.99	96,562.74	105,376.90
1,145.41	59.08	96	1,086.33	96,503.66	106,463.23
Payments 97 through 111 omitted to conserve space.					
1,145.41	70.66	112	1,074.75	95,462.68	123,748.84
Four First-Day Payments					
1,145.41	71.46	113	1,073.96	95,391.22	124,822.80
1,145.41	72.26	114	1,073.15	95,318.96	125,895.95
Payments 115 through 125 omitted to conserve space.					
1,145.41	82.64	126	1,062.77	94,385.73	138,707.66
Five First-Day Payments					
1,145.41	83.57	127	1,061.84	94,302.15	139,769.50
1,145.41	84.51	128	1,060.90	94,217.64	140,830.40

This illustration shows the effect of 1 through 5 first-day payments on a standard amortization schedule. The boxed number is how many payments are eliminated by making the first-day payment. The underlined number is the balance after making the first-day payment. The circled number is the interest saved.

Support Information
The First-Day Payment Strategy
13% Interest Rate

Loan Amount	$100,000.00
Term	30 Years
Payment	$1,106.20

Pmt. No.	Pmt. Amt.	Mos. Saved	Yrs. Saved	Int. Saved	Yrs. to Payoff
1	$1,106.20	39	3yrs.3mo.	$42,039.33	26yrs.9mo.
2	2,212.40	67	5yrs.7mo.	71,881.37	24yrs.5mo.
3	3,318.60	88	7yrs.4mo.	94,008.34	22yrs.8mo.
4	4,424.80	105	8yrs.9mo.	111,718.55	21yrs.3mo.
5	5,531.00	119	9yrs.11mo.	126,139.97	20yrs.1mo.

This illustration shows what will happen when 1 through 5 payments are made before any interest is due. This strategy also works on existing mortgages.

Support Information
The First-Day Payment Strategy
13% Interest Continued

Pmt. Amt.	Prin.	Pmt. No.	Int.	Bal.	Total Int.
$1,106.20	22.87	1	$1,083.33	$99,977.13	
1,106.20	23.11	2	1,083.09	99,954.02	$2,166.42
1,106.20	23.36	3	1,082.84	99,930.66	3,249.25
Payments 4 through 37 omitted to conserve space.					
1,106.20	34.07	38	1,072.13	98,931.99	40,967.57
One First-Day Payment					
1,106.20	34.44	39	1,071.76	98,897.55	42,039.33
1,106.20	34.81	40	1,071.39	98,862.74	43,110.72
Payments 41 through 65 omitted to conserve space.					
1,106.20	46.06	66	1,060.14	97,812.57	70,821.74
Two First-Day Payments					
1,106.20	46.56	67	1,059.64	97,766.00	71,881.37
1,106.20	47.07	68	1,059.13	97,718.94	72,940.50
Payments 69 through 86 omitted to conserve space.					
1,106.20	57.76	87	1,048.44	96,721.17	92,960.53
Three First-Day Payments					
1,106.20	58.39	88	1,047.81	96,662.78	94,008.34
1,106.20	59.02	89	1,047.18	96,603.76	95,055.52
Payments 90 through 103 omitted to conserve space.					
1,106.20	69.37	104	1,036.83	95,637.73	110,682.48
Four First-Day Payments					
1,106.20	70.12	105	1,036.08	95,567.60	111,718.55
1,106.20	70.88	106	1,035.32	95,496.72	112,753.87
Payments 107 through 117 omitted to conserve space.					
1,106.20	80.67	118	1,025.53	94,583.77	125,115.32
Five First-Day Payments					
1,106.20	81.54	119	1,024.66	94,502.23	126,139.97
1,106.20	82.43	120	1,023.77	94,419.81	127,163.75

This illustration shows the effect of 1 through 5 first-day payments on a standard amortization schedule. The boxed number is how many payments are eliminated by making the first-day payment. The underlined number is the balance after making the first-day payment. The circled number is the interest saved.

Support Information
The First-Day Payment Strategy
12.5% Interest Rate

Loan Amount	$100,000.00
Term	30 Years
Payment	$1,067.26

Pmt. No.	Pmt. Amt.	Mos. Saved	Yrs. Saved	Int. Saved	Yrs. to Payoff
1	$1,067.26	35	2yrs.11mo.	$36,279.93	27yrs.1mo.
2	2,134.52	60	5yrs.	61,917.22	25yrs
3	3,201.78	81	6yrs.9mo.	83,217.39	23yrs.3mo.
4	4,269.04	97	8yrs.1mo.	99,267.87	21yrs.11mo.
5	5,336.30	111	9yrs.3mo.	113,161.39	20yrs.9mo.

This illustration shows what will happen when 1 through 5 payments are made before any interest is due. This strategy also works on existing mortgages.

Support Information
The First-Day Payment Strategy
12.5% Interest Continued

Pmt. Amt.	Prin.	Pmt. No.	Int.	Bal.	Total Int.
$1,067.26	25.59	1	$1,041.67	$99,974.41	
1,067.26	25.86	2	1,041.40	99,948.55	$2,083.07
1,067.26	26.13	3	1,041.13	99,922.42	3,124.20
Payments 4 through 33 omitted to conserve space.					
1,067.26	36.03	34	1,031.23	$98,962.31	35,249.07
One First-Day Payment					
1,067.26	36.40	35	1,030.86	98,925.91	36,279.93
1,067.26	36.78	36	1,030.48	98,889.13	37,310.41
Payments 37 through 58 omitted to conserve space.					
1,067.26	46.68	59	1,020.58	97,928.92	60,897.13
Two First-Day Payments					
1,067.26	47.16	60	1,020.09	97,881.75	61,917.22
1,067.26	47.66	61	1,019.60	97,834.10	62,936.82
Payments 62 through 79 omitted to conserve space.					
1,067.26	58.03	80	1,009.23	96,828.15	82,208.77
Three First-Day Payments					
1,067.26	58.63	81	1,008.63	96,769.52	83,217.39
1,067.26	59.24	82	1,008.02	96,710.27	84,225.41
Payments 83 through 95 omitted to conserve space.					
1,067.26	68.49	96	998.77	95,813.07	98,269.82
Four First-Day Payments					
1,067.26	69.20	97	998.05	95,743.87	99,267.87
1,067.26	69.93	98	997.33	95,673.94	100,265.20
Payments 99 through 109 omitted to conserve space.					
1,067.26	79.19	110	988.07	94,775.79	112,174.14
Five First-Day Payments					
1,067.26	80.01	111	987.25	94,695.78	113,161.39
1,067.26	80.84	112	986.41	94,614.94	114,147.81

This illustration shows the effect of 1 through 5 first-day
payments on a standard amortization schedule. The boxed
number is how many payments are eliminated by making the
first-day payment. The underlined number is the balance after
making the first-day payment. The circled number is the
interest saved.

Support Information
The First-Day Payment Strategy
12% Interest Rate

Loan Amount	$100,000.00
Term	30 Years
Payment	$1,028.61

Pmt. No.	Pmt. Amt.	Mos. Saved	Yrs. Saved	Int. Saved	Yrs. to Payoff
1	$1,028.61	31	2yrs.7mo.	$30,853.14	27yrs.5mo.
2	2,057.22	54	4yrs.6mo.	53,509.55	25yrs.6mo.
3	3,085.83	74	6yrs.2mo.	73,003.58	23yrs.10mo.
4	4,114.44	90	7yrs.6mo.	88,430.22	22yrs.6mo.
5	5,143.05	103	8yrs.5mo.	100,834.68	21yrs.6mo.

This illustration shows what will happen when 1 through 5 payments are made before any interest is due. This strategy also works on existing mortgages.

Support Information
The First-Day Payment Strategy
12% Interest Continued

Pmt. Amt.	Prin.	Pmt. No.	Int.	Bal.	Total Int.
$1,028.61	28.61	1	$1,000.00	$99,971.39	
1,028.61	28.90	2	999.71	99,942.49	$1,999.71
1,028.61	29.19	3	999.42	99,913.30	2,999.14
Payments 4 through 29 omitted to conserve space.					
1,028.61	38.18	30	990.43	99,004.71	29,863.09
One First-Day Payment					
1,028.61	38.57	31	990.05	98,966.15	30,853.14
1,028.61	38.95	32	989.66	98,927.20	31,842.80
Payments 33 through 52 omitted to conserve space.					
1,028.61	48.00	53	980.61	98,012.95	52,529.42
Two First-Day Payments					
1,028.61	48.48	54	980.13	97,964.47	53,509.55
1,028.61	48.97	55	979.64	97,915.50	54,489.19
Payments 56 through 72 omitted to conserve space.					
1,028.61	58.57	73	970.04	96,945.40	72,034.12
Three First-Day Payments					
1,028.61	59.16	74	969.45	96,886.25	73,003.58
1,028.61	59.75	75	968.86	96,826.50	73,972.44
Payments 76 through 88 omitted to conserve space.					
1,028.61	68.68	89	959.93	95,924.45	87,470.97
Four First-Day Payments					
1,028.61	69.37	90	959.24	95,855.09	88,430.22
1,028.61	70.06	91	958.55	95,785.02	89,388.77
Payments 92 through 101 omitted to conserve space.					
1,028.61	78.17	102	950.45	94,966.53	99,885.01
Five First-Day Payments					
1,028.61	78.95	103	949.67	94,887.58	100,834.68
1,028.61	79.74	104	948.88	94,807.84	101,783.55

This illustration shows the effect of 1 through 5 first-day payments on a standard amortization schedule. The boxed number is how many payments are eliminated by making the first-day payment. The underlined number is the balance after making the first-day payment. The circled number is the interest saved.

Support Information
The First-Day Payment Strategy
11.5% Interest Rate

Loan Amount		$100,000.00
Term		30 Years
Payment		$990.29

Pmt. No.	Pmt. Amt.	Mos. Saved	Yrs. Saved	Int. Saved	Yrs. to Payoff
1	$990.29	27	2yrs.3mo.	$25,758.40	27yrs.9mo.
2	1,980.58	49	4yrs.1mo.	46,537.58	25yrs.11mo.
3	2,970.87	67	5yrs.7mo.	63,366.13	24yrs.5mo.
4	3,961.16	82	6yrs.10mo.	77,248.74	23yrs.2mo.
5	4,951.45	96	8yrs.	90,071.43	22yrs.

This illustration shows what will happen when 1 through 5 payments are made before any interest is due. This strategy also works on existing mortgages.

Support Information
The First-Day Payment Strategy
11.5% Interest Continued

Pmt. Amt.	Prin.	Pmt. No.	Int.	Bal.	Total Int.
$990.29	31.96	1	$958.33	$99,968.04	
990.29	32.26	2	958.03	99,935.78	$1,916.36
990.29	32.57	3	957.72	99,903.20	2,874.08

Payments 4 through 25 omitted to conserve space.

990.29	40.56	26	949.73	99,061.48	24,809.06

One First-Day Payment

990.29	40.95	27	949.34	99,020.53	25,758.40
990.29	41.34	28	948.95	98,979.19	26,707.35

Payments 29 through 47 omitted to conserve space.

990.29	50.03	48	940.26	98,063.81	45,597.80

Two First-Day Payments

990.29	50.51	49	939.78	98,013.30	46,537.58
990.29	51.00	50	939.29	97,962.30	47,476.87

Payments 51 through 65 omitted to conserve space.

990.29	59.40	66	930.89	97,076.58	62,435.82

Three First-Day Payments

990.29	59.97	67	930.32	97,016.61	63,366.13
990.29	60.55	68	929.74	96,956.06	64,295.88

Payments 69 through 80 omitted to conserve space.

990.29	68.54	81	921.75	96,114.04	76,327.6

Four First-Day Payments

990.29	69.20	82	921.09	96,044.84	77,248.74
990.29	69.86	83	920.43	95,974.98	78,169.17

Payments 84 through 94 omitted to conserve space.

990.29	78.33	95	911.96	95,082.54	89,160.23

Five First-Day Payments

990.29	79.08	96	911.21	95,003.46	90,071.43
990.29	79.84	97	910.45	94,923.61	90,981.88

This illustration shows the effect of 1 through 5 first-day
payments on a standard amortization schedule. The boxed
number is how many payments are eliminated by making the
first-day payment. The underlined number is the balance after
making the first-day payment. The circled number is the
interest saved.

Support Information
The First-Day Payment Strategy
11% Interest Rate

Loan Amount	$100,000.00
Term	30 Years
Payment	$952.32

Pmt. No.	Pmt. Amt.	Mos. Saved	Yrs. Saved	Int. Saved	Yrs. to Payoff
1	$952.32	24	2yrs.	$21,903.42	28yrs.
2	1,904.64	44	3yrs.8mo.	39,980.43	26yrs.4mo.
3	2,856.96	60	5yrs.	54,304.05	25yrs.
4	3,809.28	75	6yrs.3mo.	67,602.43	23yrs.9mo.
5	4,761.60	88	7yrs.4mo.	79,011.38	22yrs.8mo.

This illustration shows what will happen when 1 through 5 payments are made before any interest is due. This strategy also works on exsiting mortgages.

Support Information
The First-Day Payment Strategy
11% Interest Continued

Pmt. Amt.	Prin.	Pmt. No.	Int.	Bal.	Total Int.
$952.32	35.66	1	$916.67	$99,964.34	
952.32	35.98	2	916.34	99,928.36	$1,833.01
952.32	36.31	3	916.01	99,892.05	2,749.02

Payments 4 through 22 omitted to conserve space.

952.32	43.58	23	908.74	99,091.64	20,995.08

One First-Day Payment

952.32	43.98	24	908.34	99,047.66	21,903.42
952.32	44.39	25	907.94	99,003.27	22,811.36

Payments 26 through 42 omitted to conserve space.

952.32	52.31	43	900.01	98,130.99	39,080.90

Two First-Day Payments

952.32	52.79	44	899.53	98,078.20	39,980.43
952.32	53.27	45	899.05	98,024.93	40,879.48

Payments 46 through 58 omitted to conserve space.

952.32	60.53	59	891.79	97,225.73	53,412.81

Three First-Day Payments

952.32	61.09	60	891.24	97,164.65	54,304.05
952.32	61.65	61	890.68	97,103.00	55,194.73

Payments 62 through 73 omitted to conserve space.

952.32	69.41	74	882.91	96,248.22	66,720.15

Four First-Day Payments

952.32	70.05	75	882.28	96,178.17	67,602.43
952.32	70.69	76	881.63	96,107.48	68,484.06

Payments 77 through 86 omitted to conserve space.

952.32	78.15	87	874.17	95,285.79	78,137.93

Five First-Day Payments

952.32	78.87	88	873.45	95,206.92	79,011.38
952.32	79.59	89	872.73	95,127.33	79,884.11

This illustration shows the effect of 1 through 5 first-day
payments on a standard amortization schedule. The boxed
number is how many payments are eliminated by making the
first-day payment. The underlined number is the balance after
making the first-day payment. The circled number is the
interest saved.

Support Information
The First-Day Payment Strategy
10.5% Interest Rate

Loan Amount		$100,000.00
Term		30 Years
Payment		$914.74

Pmt. No.	Pmt. Amt.	Mos. Saved	Yrs. Saved	Int. Saved	Yrs. to Payoff
1	$914.74	21	1yr.9mo.	$18,297.77	28yrs.3mo.
2	1,829.48	39	3yrs.3mo.	33,837.20	26yrs.9mo.
3	2,744.22	54	4yrs.6mo.	46,667.74	25yrs.6mo.
4	3,658.96	68	5yrs.8mo.	58,531.07	24yrs.4mo.
5	4,573.70	80	6yrs.8mo.	68,602.85	23yrs.4mo.

This illustration shows what will happen when 1 through 5 payments are made before any interest is due. This strategy also works on existing mortgages.

Support Information
The First-Day Payment Strategy
10.5% Interest Continued

Pmt. Amt.	Prin.	Pmt. No.	Int.	Bal.	Total Int.
$914.74	39.74	1	875.00	$99,960.26	
914.74	40.09	2	874.65	99,920.17	$1,749.65
914.74	40.44	3	874.30	99,879.74	2,623.95
Payments 4 through 19 omitted to conserve space.					
914.74	46.89	20	867.85	99,135.55	17,430.33
One First-Day Payment					
914.74	47.30	21	867.44	99,088.24	18,297.77
914.74	47.72	22	867.02	99,040.53	19,164.79
Payments 23 through 37 omitted to conserve space.					
914.74	54.85	38	859.88	98,217.71	32,977.80
Two First-Day Payments					
914.74	55.33	39	859.40	98,162.37	33,837.20
914.74	55.82	40	858.92	98,106.55	34,696.12
Payments 41 through 52 omitted to conserve space.					
914.74	62.51	53	852.23	97,334.87	45,816.06
Three First-Day Payments					
914.74	63.06	54	851.68	97,271.81	46,667.74
914.74	63.61	55	851.13	97,208.20	47,518.86
Payments 56 through 66 omitted to conserve space.					
914.74	70.62	67	844.12	96,400.03	57,687.57
Four First-Day Payments					
914.74	71.24	68	843.50	96,328.79	58,531.07
914.74	71.86	69	842.88	96,256.93	59,373.94
Payments 70 through 78 omitted to conserve space.					
914.74	78.40	79	836.34	95,502.80	67,767.20
Five First-Day Payments					
914.74	79.09	80	835.65	95,423.71	68,602.85
914.74	79.78	81	834.96	95,343.93	69,437.81

This illustration shows the effect of 1 through 5 first-day payments on a standard amortization schedule. The boxed number is how many payments are eliminated by making the first-day payment. The underlined number is the balance after making the first-day payment. The circled number is the interest saved.

Support Information
The First-Day Payment Strategy
10% Interest Rate

Loan Amount	$100,000.00
Term	30 Years
Payment	$877.57

Pmt. No.	Pmt. Amt.	Mos. Saved	Yrs. Saved	Int. Saved	Yrs. to Payoff
1	$877.57	18	1yr.6mo.	$14,941.01	28yrs.6mo.
2	1,755.14	34	2yrs.10mo.	28,106.89	27yrs.2mo.
3	2,632.71	49	4yrs.1mo.	40,337.34	25yrs.11mo.
4	3,510.28	61	5yrs.1mo.	50,033.40	24yrs.11mo.
5	4,387.85	73	6yrs.1mo.	59,642.05	23yrs.11mo.

This illustration shows what will happen when 1 through 5 payments are made before any interest is due. This strategy also works on existing mortgages.

Support Information
The First-Day Payment Strategy
10% Interest Continued

Pmt. Amt.	Prin.	Pmt. No.	Int.	Bal.	Total Int.
$877.57	44.24	1	833.33	$99,955.76	
877.57	44.61	2	832.96	99,911.15	$1,666.30
877.57	44.98	3	832.59	99,866.18	2,498.89
Payments 4 through 16 omitted to conserve space.					
877.57	50.52	17	827.05	99,195.66	14,114.38
One First-Day Payment					
877.57	50.94	18	826.63	99,144.72	14,941.01
877.57	51.37	19	826.21	99,093.36	15,767.22
Payments 20 through 32 omitted to conserve space.					
877.57	57.69	33	819.88	98,327.63	27,287.49
Two First-Day Payments					
877.57	58.17	34	819.40	98,269.45	28,106.89
877.57	58.66	35	818.91	98,210.79	28,925.80
Payments 36 through 47 omitted to conserve space.					
877.57	65.34	48	812.23	97,402.22	39,525.66
Three First-Day Payments					
877.57	65.89	49	811.69	97,336.33	40,337.34
877.57	66.44	50	811.14	97,269.90	41,148.48
Payments 51 through 59 omitted to conserve space.					
877.57	72.18	60	805.39	96,574.32	49,228.61
Four First-Day Payments					
877.57	72.79	61	804.79	96,501.53	50,033.40
877.57	73.39	62	804.18	96,428.14	50,837.58
Payments 63 through 71 omitted to conserve space.					
877.57	79.74	72	797.83	95,659.73	58,844.88
Five First-Day Payments					
877.57	80.41	73	797.16	95,579.32	59,642.05
877.57	81.08	74	796.49	95,498.24	60,438.54

This illustration shows the effect of 1 through 5 first-day payments on a standard amortization schedule. The boxed number is how many payments are eliminated by making the first-day payment. The underlined number is the balance after making the first-day payment. The circled number is the interest saved.

Support Information
The First-Day Payment Strategy
9.5% Interest Rate

Loan Amount	$100,000.00
Term	30 Years
Payment	$840.85

Pmt. No.	Pmt. Amt.	Mos. Saved	Yrs. Saved	Int. Saved	Yrs. to Payoff
1	$840.85	16	1yr.4mo.	$12,618.17	28yrs.8mo.
2	1,681.70	30	2yrs.6mo.	23,567.40	27yrs.6mo.
3	2,522.55	43	3yrs.7mo.	33,648.79	26yrs.5mo.
4	3,363.40	55	4yrs.7mo.	42,873.49	25yrs.5mo.
5	4,204.25	66	5yrs.6mo.	51,254.20	24yrs.6mo.

This illustration shows what will happen when 1 through 5 payments are made before any interest is due. This strategy also works on existing mortgages.

Support Information
The First-Day Payment Strategy
9.5% Interest Continued

Pmt. Amt.	Pmt. Prin.	No.	Int.	Bal.	Total Int.
$840.85	49.19	1	$791.67	$99,950.81	
840.85	49.58	2	791.28	99,901.24	$1,582.94
840.85	49.97	3	790.88	99,851.27	2,373.83

Payments 4 through 14 omitted to conserve space.

840.85	54.93	15	785.93	99,219.86	11,832.68

One First-Day Payment

840.85	55.36	16	785.49	99,164.50	12,618.17
840.85	55.80	17	785.05	99,108.70	13,403.22

Payments 18 through 28 omitted to conserve space.

840.85	61.34	29	779.51	98,403.60	22,788.37

Two First-Day Payments

840.85	61.83	30	779.03	98,341.77	23,567.40
840.85	62.32	31	778.54	98,279.46	24,345.94

Payments 32 through 41 omitted to conserve space.

840.85	67.96	42	772.89	97,560.55	32,876.43

Three First-Day Payments

840.85	68.50	43	772.35	97,492.05	33,648.79
840.85	69.04	44	771.81	97,423.01	34,420.60

Payments 45 through 53 omitted to conserve space.

840.85	74.71	54	766.15	96,701.80	42,107.93

Four First-Day Payments

840.85	75.30	55	765.56	96,626.51	42,873.49
840.85	75.89	56	764.96	96,550.61	43,638.45

Payments 57 through 64 omitted to conserve space.

840.85	81.48	65	759.38	95,839.95	50,495.47

Five First-Day Payments

840.85	82.12	66	758.73	95,757.82	51,254.20
840.85	82.77	67	758.08	95,675.05	52,012.28

This illustration shows the effect of 1 through 5 first-day
payments on a standard amortization schedule. The boxed
number is how many payments are eliminated by making the
first-day payment. The underlined number is the balance after
making the first-day payment. The circled number is the
interest saved.

Support Information
The First-Day Payment Strategy
9% Interest Rate

Loan Amount	$100,000.00
Term	30 Years
Payment	$804.62

Pmt. No.	Pmt. Amt.	Mos. Saved	Yrs. Saved	Int. Saved	Yrs. to Payoff
1	$804.62	14	1yr.2mo.	$10,461.58	28yrs.10mo.
2	1,609.24	27	2yrs.3mo.	20,096.80	27yrs.9mo.
3	2,413.86	38	3yrs.2mo	28,184.29	26yrs.10mo.
4	3,218.48	49	4yrs.1mo.	36,206.33	25yrs.11mo.
5	4,023.10	59	4yrs.11mo.	43,437.68	25yrs.1mo.

This illustration shows what will happen when 1 through 5 payments are made before any interest is due. This strategy also works on existing mortgages.

Support Information
The First-Day Payment Strategy
9% Interest Continued

Pmt. Amt.	Prin.	Pmt. No.	Int.	Bal.	Total Int.
$804.62	54.62	1	$750.00	$99,945.38	
804.62	55.03	2	749.59	99,890.35	$1,499.59
804.62	55.45	3	749.18	99,834.90	2,248.77
Payments 4 through 12 omitted to conserve space.					
804.62	59.75	13	744.88	99,257.06	9,717.15
One First-Day Payment					
804.62	60.19	14	744.43	99,196.86	10,461.58
804.62	60.65	15	743.98	99,136.22	11,205.55
Payments 16 through 25 omitted to conserve space.					
804.62	65.84	26	738.78	98,438.32	19,358.51
Two First-Day Payments					
804.62	66.34	27	738.29	98,371.99	20,096.80
804.62	66.83	28	737.79	98,305.16	20,834.59
Payments 29 through 36 omitted to conserve space.					
804.62	71.48	37	733.14	97,680.65	27,451.69
Three First-Day Payments					
804.62	72.02	38	732.60	97,608.63	28,184.29
804.62	72.56	39	732.06	97,536.07	28,916.36
Payments 40 through 47 omitted to conserve space.					
804.62	77.61	48	727.02	96,858.07	35,479.95
Four First-Day Payments					
804.62	78.19	49	726.44	96,779.88	36,206.39
804.62	78.77	50	725.85	96,701.11	36,932.24
Payments 51 through 57 omitted to conserve space.					
804.62	83.63	58	721.00	96,049.27	42,717.39
Five First-Day Payments					
804.62	84.25	59	720.37	95,965.02	43,437.76
804.62	84.88	60	719.74	95,880.14	44,157.49

This illustration shows the effect of 1 through 5 first-day
payments on a standard amortization schedule. The boxed
number is how many payments are eliminated by making the
first-day payment. The underlined number is the balance after
making the first-day payment. The circled number is the
interest saved.

Support Information
The First-Day Payment Strategy
8.5% Interest Rate

Loan Amount	$100,000.00
Term	30 Years
Payment	$768.91

Pmt. No.	Pmt. Amt.	Mos. Saved	Yrs. Saved	Int. Saved	Yrs. to Payoff
1	$768.91	12	1yr.	$8,471.00	29yrs.
2	1,537.82	23	1yr.11mo.	16,177.52	28yrs.1mo
3	2,306.73	34	2yrs.10mo.	23,823.37	27yrs.2mo.
4	3,075.64	44	3yrs.8mo.	30,717.38	26yrs.4mo.
5	3,844.55	53	4yrs.5mo.	36,872.38	25yrs.7mo.

This illustration shows what will happen when 1 through 5 payments are made before any interest is due. This strategy also works on existing mortgages.

Support Information
The First-Day Payment Strategy
8.5% Interest Continued

Pmt. Amt.	Prin.	Pmt. No.	Int.	Bal.	Total Int.
$768.91	60.58	1	$708.33	$99,939.42	
768.91	61.01	2	707.90	99,878.41	$1,416.24
768.91	61.44	3	707.47	99,816.97	2,123.71

Payments 4 through 10 omitted to conserve space.

768.91	65.01	11	703.90	99,309.51	7,767.56

One First-Day Payment

768.91	65.47	12	703.44	99,244.04	8,471.00
768.91	65.93	13	702.98	99,178.10	9,173.98

Payments 14 through 21 omitted to conserve space.

768.91	70.26	22	698.65	98,563.27	15,479.37

Two First-Day Payments

768.91	70.76	23	698.16	98,492.51	16,177.52
768.91	71.26	24	697.66	98,421.25	16,875.18

Payments 25 through 32 omitted to conserve space.

768.91	75.93	33	692.98	97,756.78	23,130.93

Three First-Day Payments

768.91	76.47	34	692.44	97,680.31	23,823.37
768.91	77.01	35	691.90	97,603.30	24,515.27

Payments 36 through 42 omitted to conserve space.

768.91	81.48	43	687.43	96,967.25	30,030.53

Four First-Day Payments

768.91	82.06	44	686.85	96,885.18	30,717.38
768.91	82.64	45	686.27	96,802.54	31,403.65

Payments 46 through 51 omitted to conserve space.

768.91	86.83	52	682.08	96,207.41	36,190.91

Five First-Day Payments

768.91	87.44	53	681.47	96,119.97	36,872.38
768.91	88.06	54	680.85	96,031.90	37,553.23

This illustration shows the effect of 1 through 5 first-day payments on a standard amortization schedule. The boxed number is how many payments are eliminated by making the first-day payment. The underlined number is the balance after making the first-day payment. The circled number is the interest saved.

Support Information
The First-Day Payment Strategy
8% Interest Rate

Loan Amount	$100,000.00
Term	30 Years
Payment	$733.76

Pmt. No.	Pmt. Amt.	Mos. Saved	Yrs. Saved	Int. Saved	Yrs. to Payoff
1	$733.76	11		$7,308.23	29yrs.1mo.
2	1,467.52	20	1yr.8mos.	13,244.84	28yrs.3mo.
3	2,201.28	30	2yrs.6mo.	19,792.74	27yrs.6mo.
4	2,935.04	39	3yrs.3mo.	25,639.57	26yrs.10mo.
5	3,668.80	47	3yrs.11mo.	30,797.67	26yrs.1mo.

This illustration shows what will happen when 1 through 5 payments are made before any interest is due. This strategy also works on existing mortgages.

Support Information
The First-Day Payment Strategy
8% Interest Continued

Pmt. Amt.	Prin.	Pmt. No.	Int.	Bal.	Total Int.
$733.76	67.10	1	$666.67	$99,932.90	
733.76	67.55	2	666.22	99,865.36	$1,332.89
733.76	68.00	3	665.77	99,797.36	1,998.66
Payments 4 through 9 omitted to conserve space.					
733.76	71.23	10	662.53	99,308.53	6,646.18
One First-Day Payment					
733.76	71.71	11	662.06	99,236.82	7,308.23
733.76	72.19	12	661.58	99,164.64	7,969.81
Payments 13 through 18 omitted to conserve space.					
733.76	75.62	19	658.14	98,645.68	12,587.21
Two First-Day Payments					
733.76	76.13	20	657.64	98,569.55	13,244.84
733.76	76.63	21	657.13	98,492.92	13,901.97
Payments 22 through 28 omitted to conserve space.					
733.76	80.82	29	652.95	97,861.16	19,140.34
Three First-Day Payments					
733.76	81.36	30	652.41	97,779.81	19,792.74
733.76	81.90	31	651.87	97,697.91	20,444.61
Payments 32 through 37 omitted to conserve space.					
733.76	85.80	38	647.97	97,109.12	24,992.17
Four First-Day Payments					
733.76	86.37	39	647.39	97,022.75	25,639.57
733.76	86.95	40	646.82	96,935.80	26,286.39
Payments 41 through 45 omitted to conserve space.					
733.76	90.48	46	643.28	96,401.82	30,154.99
Five First-Day Payments					
733.76	91.09	47	642.68	96,310.73	30,797.67
733.76	91.69	48	642.07	96,219.04	31,439.74

This illustration shows the effect of 1 through 5 first-day payments on a standard amortization schedule. The boxed number is how many payments are eliminated by making the first-day payment. The underlined number is the balance after making the first-day payment. The circled number is the interest saved.

Support Information
The First-Day Payment Strategy
7.5% Interest Rate

Loan Amount	$100,000.00
Term	30 Years
Payment	$699.21

Pmt. No.	Pmt. Amt.	Mos. Saved	Yrs. Saved	Int. Saved	Yrs. to Payoff
1	$699.21	9		$5,608.06	29yrs.3mo.
2	1,398.42	18	1yr.6mo.	11,176.61	28yrs.6mo.
3	2,097.63	26	2yrs.2mo.	16,091.44	27yrs.10mo.
4	2,796.84	34	2yrs10mo.	2,0971.56	27yrs.2mo.
5	3,496.05	41	3yrs.6mo.	25,211.82	26yrs.6mo.

This illustration shows what will happen when 1 through 5 payments are made before any interest is due. This strategy also works on existing mortgages.

Support Information
The First-Day Payment Strategy
7.5% Interest Continued

Pmt. Amt.	Prin.	Pmt. No.	Int.	Bal.	Total Int.
$699.21	74.21	1	$625.00	$99,925.79	
699.21	74.68	2	624.54	99,851.11	$1,249.54
699.21	75.15	3	624.07	99,775.96	1,873.61
699.21	75.61	4	623.60	99,700.35	2,497.21

Payments 5 through 8 omitted to conserve space.

One First-Day Payment

699.21	78.01	9	621.21	99,315.13	5,608.06
699.21	78.49	10	620.72	99,236.63	6,228.78

Payments 11 through 16 omitted to conserve space.

699.21	81.99	17	617.22	98,673.26	10,559.90

Two First-Day Payments

699.21	82.51	18	616.71	98,590.75	11,176.61
699.21	83.02	19	616.19	98,507.73	11,792.80

Payments 20 through 24 omitted to conserve space.

699.21	86.18	25	613.03	97,998.58	15,478.94

Three First-Day Payments

699.21	86.72	26	612.49	97,911.86	16,091.44
699.21	87.27	27	611.95	97,824.59	16,703.38

Payments 28 through 32 omitted to conserve space.

699.21	90.59	33	608.63	97,289.43	20,363.51

Four First-Day payments

699.21	91.16	34	608.06	97,198.27	20,971.56
699.21	91.73	35	607.49	97,106.55	21,579.05

Payments 36 through 39 omitted to conserve space.

699.21	94.63	40	604.59	96,639.25	24,607.83

Five First-Day Payments

699.21	95.22	41	604.00	96,544.03	25,211.82
699.21	95.81	42	603.40	96,448.22	25,815.22

This illustration shows the effect of 1 through 5 first-day payments on a standard amortization schedule. The boxed number is how many payments are eliminated by making the first-day payment. The underlined number is the balance after making the first-day payment. The circled number is the interest saved.

Support Information
The First-Day Payment Strategy
7% Interest Rate

Loan Amount	$100,000.00
Term	30 Years
Payment	$665.30

Pmt. No.	Pmt. Amt.	Mos. Saved	Yrs. Saved	Int. Saved	Yrs. to Payoff
1	$665.30	8		$4,653.12	29yrs.4mo.
2	1,330.60	16	1yr.4mo.	9,274.36	28yrs.8mo.
3	1,995.90	22	1yr.10mo.	12,718.46	28yrs.2mo.
4	2,661.20	30	2yrs.6mo.	17,280.22	27yrs.6mo.
5	3,326.50	37	3yrs.1mo.	21,242.09	26yrs.11mo.

This illustration shows what will happen when 1 through 5 payments are made before any interest is due. This strategy also works on existing mortgages.

Support Information
The First-Day Payment Strategy
7% Interest Continued

Pmt. Amt.	Prin.	Pmt. No.	Int.	Bal.	Total Int.
$665.30	81.97	1	$583.33	$99,918.03	
665.30	82.45	2	582.86	99,835.58	1,166.19
665.30	82.93	3	582.37	99,752.66	1,748.56
665.30	83.41	4	581.89	99,669.24	2,330.45

Payments 5 through 7 omitted to conserve space.

One First-Day Payment

665.30	85.38	8	579.93	99,330.70	4,653.12
665.30	85.87	9	579.43	99,244.83	5,232.55

Payments 10 through 14 omitted to conserve space.

665.30	88.92	15	576.38	98,718.96	8,698.50

Two First-Day Payments

665.30	89.44	16	575.86	98,629.52	9,274.36
665.30	89.96	17	575.34	98,539.56	9,849.70

Payments 18 through 20 omitted to conserve space

665.30	92.08	21	573.22	98,174.43	12,145.78

Three First-Day Payments

665.30	92.62	22	572.68	98,081.81	12,718.46
665.30	93.16	23	572.14	97,988.65	13,290.61

Payments 24 through 28 omitted to conserve space.

665.30	96.47	29	568.84	97,418.17	16,711.95

Four First-Day Payments

665.30	97.03	30	568.27	97,321.14	17,280.22
665.30	97.60	31	567.71	97,223.55	17,847.93

Payments 32 through 35 omitted to conserve space.

665.30	100.48	36	564.83	96,726.96	20,677.85

Five First-Day Payments

665.30	101.06	37	564.24	96,625.90	21,242.09
665.30	101.65	38	563.65	96,524.25	21,805.74

This illustration shows the effect of 1 through 5 first-day payments on a standard amortization schedule. The boxed number is how many payments are eliminated by making the first-day payment. The underlined number is the balance after making the first-day payment. The circled number is the interest saved.

6

The Split-Payment Strategy

Another explosive way to rapidly pay off a mortgage is to make half payments every **fourteen days.** Pay close attention to what I just said. **I did not say** you must make half-payments twice a month; I said you must make a **half payment every two weeks** (fourteen days).

The power behind this strategy is twofold. Following this plan will cause you to automatically make **one extra payment every year.** You will also be lowering the principal balance of your loan **twenty-six times instead of the standard twelve times** per year. This may seem too simple for it to do much good, but the effect it will have on your mortgage is most impressive. This simple plan can **quickly take a substantial number of years off the term of your loan.** It will also save you many thousands of dollars in interest.

How It Works

This is how it works. As you know, there are fifty-two weeks in each year. If **a half payment** is made every two weeks, you will make **twenty-six** half payments each year. Figure it out. Twenty-six half payments are equal to **thirteen** whole payments. If you pay one full payment each month, you will make only twelve payments each year.

Also, with the split-payment schedule, you will be making a paydown on the balance of your note every fourteen days. This means you will be paying interest on a rapidly decreasing principal amount. These two factors reduce your mortgage every fourteen days instead of every thirty days, and make an **all- important extra payment each and every year.**

A Bit More Each Month

In actuality you will be paying a bit more each month than you would if you made regular monthly payments. However, the additional amount you will be paying is **insignificant when compared to the tremendous amount you will save.** On a $500 monthly payment, the extra cost is only $9.62 per week.

Don't Be Stopped

If for some reason your lender refuses to let you pay every two weeks, **do not give up on this strategy.** You might still be able to operate it **without his express permission.** Here is how that is done. Instead of making your regular payment of $500, add a prepayment amount of $41.67 to your regular payment each month. That will make your total payment $541.67. If you notice, this is still the same amount that your average monthly overpayment would be if you were making your payment every two weeks.

Forcing this strategy is dependent upon there being no prepayment restriction on your mortgage. If there is a penalty, you should read it carefully, for many times this is only charged on the amount that is prepaid, not on the entire amount of the unpaid balance. In the case of the illustration, the paydown is $41.67 per month. If you had even as much as a five percent prepayment penalty, this strategy would still be profitable. Five percent of $41.67 is only $2.08. You would just add that amount to the payment and stipulate that it is the five percent penalty on your prepayment for that month.

You Can Figure It Out

You can easily figure the amount you will have to add to your own house payment in order to follow this strategy. Simply divide the amount of your regular monthly payment (payment only, not escrow costs) by twelve and add that amount to each of your regular monthly payments. This extra amount will total one extra payment each year. This will give you almost the same advantage you would have if you made half payments every two weeks.

An Example

Using the model thirty-year mortgage of $100,000 at 14.5% interest, if this mortgage is paid with the split-payment strategy, **it will save $174,697.75 in interest.** It will also reduce the amount of time it will take to pay off this mortgage **by thirteen years, and three months.** This means that by applying this strategy, **you will turn your**

thirty-year mortgage into a sixteen-year, three-month mortgage. Notice this is **almost down to one half of the original term** of the loan.

At the end of this chapter I have compared the regular thirty-day-payment mortgage with the split-payment strategy. I have carried the plan through to payoff using interest rates from 15.5% through 7%.

It Works On All Mortgages

This strategy can be applied to your mortgage, even if it is not a new one. To accurately see how this would work on your own home loan, see Chapter 15. It will give you details of how to obtain a tailor-made amortization schedule of your mortgage with this strategy applied.

Support Information
The Split-Payment Strategy
15.5% Interest Rate
30-Year Comparison

	Reg. Mo. Pmt. Amt. $1,304.52		Split-Pmt. Amt. $652.26	
Yr.	Bal.	Int.	Bal.	Int.
1	$99,834.36	$15,488.56	$98,361.73	$15,972.71
2	99,641.13	15,460.98	96,438.27	15,687.52
3	99,415.74	15,428.81	94,179.98	15,352.69
4	99,152.82	15,391.28	91,528.57	14,959.57

Years 5 through 12 omitted to conserve space.

Yr.	Bal.	Int.	Bal.	Int.
13	93,628.36	14,602.75	33,605.14	6,371.36
14	92,401.84	14,427.68	20,408.95	4,414.79
15	90,971.11	14,223.47	4,915.58	2,117.61
16	89,302.16	13,985.25	0.00	0.00
17	87,355.33	13,707.37		
18	85,084.35	13,383.23		
19	82,435.26	13,005.11		
20	79,345.09	12,564.04		
21	75,740.41	12,049.52		
22	71,535.56	11,449.35		
23	66,630.60	10,749.24		
24	60,908.96	9,932.57		
25	54,234.67	8,979.92		
26	46,449.12	7,868.65		
27	37,367.27	6,572.36		
28	26,773.30	5,060.23		
29	14,415.44	3,296.34		
30	0.00	1,238.76		
		$369,626.09		$169,209.46

> **With this strategy you will never have to make any of these payments!**

Savings With This Strategy:
Interest — $200,416.63   Time — 15 yrs. 3 mos.

Support Information
The Split-Payment Strategy
15% Interest Rate
30-Year Comparison

	Reg. Mo. Pmt. Amt. $1,264.44		Split-Pmt. Amt. $632.22	
Yr.	Bal.	Int.	Bal.	Int.
1	$99,814.24	$14,987.57	$98,389.37	$15,459.37
2	99,598.63	14,957.71	96,508.11	15,188.73
3	99,348.35	14,923.05	94,310.73	14,872.61
4	99,057.84	14,882.82	91,744.11	14,503.38

Years 5 through 12 omitted to conserve space.

Yr.	Bal.	Int.	Bal.	Int.
13	93,131.30	14,062.04	37,388.34	6,683.75
14	91,841.37	13,883.40	25,256.85	4,938.51
15	90,344.07	13,676.04	11,086.86	2,900.01
16	88,606.08	13,435.34	0.00	0.00
17	86,588.71	13,155.95		
18	84,247.02	12,831.65		
19	81,528.91	12,455.21		
20	78,373.84	12,018.26		
21	74,711.58	11,511.07		
22	70,460.60	10,922.35		
23	65,526.25	10,238.98		
24	59,798.69	9,445.76		
25	53,150.39	8,525.03		
26	45,433.35	7,456.29		
27	36,475.75	6,215.74		
28	26,078.19	4,775.76		
29	14,009.17	3,104.31		
30	0.00	1,164.16		
		$355,199.85		$167,772.70

With this strategy you will never have to pay any of these payments!

Savings With This Strategy:
Interest — $187,427.15   Time — 13 yrs. 8 mos.

Support Information
The Split-Payment Strategy
14.5% Interest Rate
30-Year Comparison

	Reg. Mo. Pmt. Amt. $1,224.56		Split-Pmt. Amt. $612.28	
Yr.	Bal.	Int.	Bal.	Int.
1	$99,791.86	$14,486.53	$98,414.20	$14,945.70
2	99,551.44	14,454.26	96,571.47	14,688.78
3	99,273.76	14,416.98	94,430.18	14,390.22
4	98,953.02	14,373.93	91,941.97	14,043.29
Years 5 through 12 omitted to conserve space.				
13	92,599.32	13,521.10	40,850.59	6,919.70
14	91,243.81	13,339.16	29,681.49	5,362.40
15	89,678.15	13,129.01	16,702.78	3,552.80
16	87,869.76	12,886.28	1,621.29	1,450.01
17	85,780.99	12,605.91	0..00	17.01
18	83,368.40	12,282.08		
19	80,581.77	11,908.04		
20	77,363.12	11,476.02		
21	73,645.45	10,977.01		
22	69,351.42	10,400.64		
23	64,391.67	9,734.91		
24	58,662.97	8,965.98		
25	52,046.13	8,077.83		
26	44,403.44	7,051.98		
27	35,575.86	5,867.09		
28	25,379.70	4,498.51		
29	13,602.77	2,917.74		
30	0.00	1,091.90		
		$340,840.13		$166,142.39

> **With this strategy you will never have to make any of these payments!**

Savings With This Strategy:
Interest — $174,697.75   Time — 13 yrs. 3 mos.

Support Information
The Split-Payment Strategy
14% Interest Rate
30-Year Comparison

	Reg. Mo. Pmt. Amt. $1,184.87		Split-Pmt. Amt. $592.44	
Yr.	Bal.	Int.	Bal.	Int.
1	$99,766.96	$13,985.42	$98,435.95	14,431.72
2	99,499.12	13,950.62	96,627.86	14,187.68
3	99,191.28	13,910.62	94,537.65	13,905.55
4	98,837.46	13,864.65	92,121.29	13,579.41
Years 5 through 12 omitted to conserve space.				
13	92,030.57	12,980.18	44,008.11	7,085.43
14	90,607.36	12,795.25	33,707.46	5,695.12
15	88,971.61	12,582.71	21,799.57	4,087.88
16	87,091.57	12,338.42	8,033.65	2,229.85
17	84,930.76	12,057.65	0.00	331.01
18	82,447.25	11,734.95		
19	79,592.85	11,364.06		
20	76,312.16	10,937.78		
21	72,541.53	10,447.83		
22	68,207.79	9,884.72		
23	63,226.84	9,237.51		
24	57,502.03	8,493.64		
25	50,922.25	7,638.69		
26	43,359.84	6,656.05		
27	34,668.05	5,526.67		
28	24,678.20	4,228.62		
29	13,196.46	2,736.71		
30	0.00	1,022.00		
		$326,553.83		$164,296.96

> **With this strategy you will never have to make any of these payments!**

Savings With This Strategy:
Interest—$162,256.87   Time—12yrs. 10 mos.

Support Information
The Split-Payment Strategy
13.5% Interest Rate
30-Year Comparison

	Reg. Mo. Pmt. Amt. $1,145.41		Split-Pmt. Amt. $572.71	
Yr.	Bal.	Int.	Bal.	Int.
1	$99,739.31	$13,484.26	$98,454.36	$13,917.42
2	99,441.18	13,446.81	96,676.75	13,685.45
3	99,100.20	13,403.97	94,632.35	13,418.67
4	98,710.24	13,354.98	92,281.15	13,111.86
Years 5 through 12 omitted to conserve space.				
13	91,423.16	12,439.54	46,875.94	7,186.77
14	89,930.20	12,251.99	37,357.55	5,944.68
15	88,222.74	12,037.49	26,410.66	4,516.18
16	86,269.96	11,792.17	13,820.89	2,873.29
17	84,036.62	11,511.61	0.00	984.29
18	81,482.41	11,190.73		
19	78,561.22	10,823.76		
20	75,220.33	10,404.06		
21	71,399.44	9,924.06		
22	67,029.58	9,375.09		
23	62,031.89	8,747.25		
24	56,316.16	8,029.21		
25	49,779.22	7,208.01		
26	42,303.09	6,268.82		
27	33,752.84	5,194.69		
28	23,974.13	3,966.24		
29	12,790.47	2,561.29		
30	0.00	954.48		
		$312,348.38		$162,214.21

With this strategy you will never have to make any of these payments!

Savings With This Strategy:
Interest — $150,134.17   Time — 12 yrs. 5 mos.

Support Information
The Split-Payment Strategy
13% Interest Rate
30-Year Comparison

	Reg. Mo. Pmt. Amt. $1,106.20		Split-Pmt. Amt. $553.10	
Yr.	Bal.	Int.	Bal.	Int.
1	$99,708.65	$12,983.05	$98,469.11	$13,402.81
2	99,377.09	12,942.83	96,717.55	13,182.13
3	98,999.76	12,897.06	94,713.49	12,929.64
4	98,570.34	12,844.98	92,420.55	12,640.75

Years 5 through 12 omitted to conserve space.

Yr.	Bal.	Int.	Bal.	Int.
13	90,775.19	11,899.50	49,468.01	7,229.15
14	89,210.51	11,709.72	40,652.85	6,118.53
15	87,429.87	11,493.75	30,566.96	4,847.81
16	85,403.43	11,247.96	19,027.17	3,393.91
17	83,097.28	10,968.24	5,823.91	1,730.43
18	80,472.81	10,649.92	0.00	<u>174.04</u>
19	77,486.07	10,287.66		
20	74,087.07	9,875.39		
21	70,218.89	9,406.22		
22	65,816.79	8,872.29		
23	60,807.04	8,264.65		
24	55,105.79	7,573.14		
25	48,617.59	6,786.19		
26	41,233.80	5,890.60		
27	32,830.80	4,871.40		
28	23,267.92	3,711.51		
29	12,385.06	2,391.53		
30	0.00	889.34		
		<u>$298,231.83</u>		<u>$159,870.73</u>

> **With this strategy you will never have to make any of these payments!**

Savings With This Strategy:
Interest — $138,361.09   Time — 12 yrs.

Support Information
The Split-Payment Strategy
12.5% Interest Rate
30-Year Comparison

	Reg. Mo. Pmt. Amt. $1,067.26		Split-Pmt. Amt. $533.63	
Yr.	Bal.	Int.	Bal.	Int.
1	$99,674.69	$12,481.78	$98,479.91	$12,887.89
2	99,306.30	12,438.70	96,749.66	12,677.73
3	98,889.13	12,389.92	94,780.19	12,438.51
4	98,416.72	12,334.68	92,538.43	12,166.22
Years 5 through 12 omitted to conserve space.				
13	90,084.79	11,360.41	51,797.29	7,217.70
14	88,446.55	11,168.85	43,612.92	6,223.61
15	86,591.37	10,951.92	34,297.02	5,092.08
16	84,490.54	10,706.26	23,693.14	3,804.10
17	82,111.53	10,428.08	11,623.23	2,338.06
18	79,417.49	10,113.06	0.00	<u>684.28</u>
19	76,366.73	9,756.33		
20	72,911.99	9,352.36		
21	68,999.79	8,894.89		
22	64,569.55	8,376.86		
23	59,552.68	7,790.22		
24	53,871.49	7,125.91		
25	47,438.03	6,373.63		
26	40,152.66	5,521.73		
27	31,902.60	4,557.03		
28	22,560.10	3,464.59		
29	11,980.51	2,227.50		
30	0.00	826.59		
		<u>$284,212.79</u>		<u>$157,243.16</u>

With this strategy you will never have to make any of these payments!

Savings With This Strategy:
Interest — $126,969.63   Time — 11 yrs. 6 mos.

Support Information
The Split-Payment Strategy
12% Interest Rate
30-Year Comparison

	Reg. Mo. Pmt. Amt. $1,028.61		Split-Pmt. Amt. $514.31	
Yr.	Bal.	Int.	Bal.	Int.
1	$99,637.12	$11,980.47	$98,486.40	12,372.67
2	99,228.22	11,934.45	96,772.43	12,172.29
3	98,767.46	11,882.59	94,831.54	11,945.38
4	98,248.26	11,824.15	92,633.70	11,688.43
Years 5 through 12 omitted to conserve space.				
13	89,350.13	10,822.66	53,875.81	7,157.23
14	87,636.58	10,629.80	46,255.92	6,266.38
15	85,705.71	10,412.48	37,627.25	5,257.60
16	83,529.96	10,167.60	27,856.25	4,115.27
17	81,078.27	9,891.66	16,791.69	2,821.71
18	78,315.64	9,580.72	4,262.31	1,356.89
19	75,202.64	9,230.35	0.00	93.97
20	71,694.83	8,835.55		
21	67,742.15	8,390.67		
22	63,288.17	7,889.37		
23	58,269.31	7,324.49		
24	52,613.94	6,687.98		
25	46,241.32	5,970.73		
26	39,060.49	5,162.53		
27	30,968.96	4,251.82		
28	21,851.22	3,225.61		
29	11,577.11	2,069.25		
30	0.00	766.24		
		$270,300.53		$154,309.14

> **With this strategy you will never have to make any of these payments!**

Savings With This Strategy:
Interest — $115,991.39   Time — 11 yrs.

Support Information
The Split-Payment Strategy
11.5% Interest Rate

30-Year Comparison

	Reg. Mo. Pmt. Amt. $990.29		Split-Pmt. Amt. $495.15	
Yr.	Bal.	Int.	Bal.	Int.
1	$99,595.63	$11,479.13	$98,488.24	$11,857.17
2	99,142.23	11,430.09	96,785.16	11,665.86
3	98,633.84	11,375.11	94,866.56	11,450.33
4	98,063.81	11,313.47	92,705.16	11,207.53

Years 5 through 12 omitted to conserve space.

Yr.	Bal.	Int.	Bal.	Int.
13	88,569.43	10,286.69	55,714.76	7,052.26
14	86,778.99	10,093.06	48,598.71	6,252.88
15	84,771.45	9,875.96	40,582.12	5,352.35
16	82,520.47	9,632.52	31,551.03	4,337.85
17	79,996.55	9,359.57	21,377.06	3,194.96
18	77,166.57	9,053.52	9,915.58	1,907.45
19	73,993.44	8,710.36	0.00	489.88
20	70,435.53	8,325.59		
21	66,446.19	7,894.16		
22	61,973.11	7,410.41		
23	56,957.62	6,868.01		
24	51,333.96	6,259.84		
25	45,028.38	5,577.92		
26	37,958.19	4,813.30		
27	30,030.67	3,955.98		
28	21,141.86	2,994.69		
29	11,175.21	1,916.84		
30	0.00	708.29		
		$256,504.92		$151,046.28

With this strategy you will never have to make any of these payments!

Savings With This Strategy:
Interest — $105,458.64   Time — 10 yrs. 6 mos..

Support Information
The Split-Payment Strategy
11% Interest Rate
30-Year Comparison

	Reg. Mo. Pmt. Amt. $952.32		Split-Pmt. Amt. $476.16	
Yr.	Bal.	Int.	Bal.	Int.
1	$99,549.87	$10,977.75	$98,485.03	$11,341.39
2	99,047.66	10,925.67	96,787.14	11,158.48
3	98,487.33	10,867.55	94,884.25	10,953.47
4	97,862.16	10,802.71	92,751.59	10,723.71
Years 5 through 12 omitted to conserve space.				
13	87,740.96	9,752.97	57,324.63	6,907.06
14	85,872.23	9,559.15	50,657.00	6,188.74
15	83,787.26	9,342.91	43,184.32	5,383.69
16	81,461.01	9,101.63	34,809.39	4,481.43
17	78,865.58	8,832.44	25,423.25	3,470.23
18	75,969.80	8,532.10	14,903.83	2,336.95
19	72,738.93	8,197.01	3,114.29	1,066.82
20	69,134.18	7,823.13	0.00	65.93
21	65,112.30	7,406.00		
22	60,625.01	6,940.59		
23	55,618.45	6,421.33		
24	50,032.54	5,841.97		
25	43,800.24	5,195.58		
26	36,846.75	4,474.38		
27	29,088.60	3,669.73		
28	20,432.69	2,771.97		
29	10,775.12	1,770.32		
30	0.00	652.76		
		$242,836.42		$147,436.05

With this strategy you will never have to make any of these payments!

Savings With This Strategy:
Interest — $95,400.37   Time — 10 yrs.

Support Information
The Split-Payment Strategy
10.5% Interest Rate
30-Year Comparison

	Reg. Mo. Pmt. Amt. **$914.74**		**Split-Pmt. Amt.** **$457.37**	
Yr.	**Bal.**	**Int.**	**Bal.**	**Int.**
1	$99,499.50	$10,476.37	$98,476.38	$10,825.36
2	98,943.84	10,421.21	96,777.60	10,650.20
3	98,326.94	10,359.97	94,883.54	10,454.91
4	97,642.06	10,291.99	92,771.72	10,237.17

Years 5 through 12 omitted to conserve space.

Yr.	Bal.	Int.	Bal.	Int.
13	86,863.13	9,222.03	58,715.19	6,725.70
14	84,914.90	9,028.64	52,445.45	6,079.24
15	82,751.96	8,813.94	45,454.94	5,358.47
16	80,350.66	8,575.57	37,660.80	4,554.84
17	77,684.74	8,310.94	28,970.64	3,658.82
18	74,725.01	8,017.15	19,281.45	2,659.80
19	71,439.12	7,690.98	8,478.40	1,545.92
20	67,791.11	7,328.86	0.00	388.06
21	63,741.07	6,926.84		
22	59,244.71	6,480.51		
23	54,252.83	5,984.99		
24	48,710.83	5,434.87		
25	42,558.09	4,824.12		
26	35,727.29	4,146.07		
27	28,143.71	3,393.29		
28	19,724.39	2,557.56		
29	10,377.24	1,629.72		
30	0.00	599.63		
		$229,306.15		**$143,461.15**

> **With this strategy you will never have to make any of these payments!**

Savings With This Strategy:
Interest—$85,845.00   Time—9 yrs. 6 mos.

Support Information
The Split-Payment Strategy
10% Interest Rate
30-Year Comparison

	Reg. Mo. Pmt. Amt. $877.57		Split-Pmt. Amt. $438.79	
Yr.	Bal.	Int.	Bal.	Int.
1	99,444.12	9,974.98	98,461.87	10,309.09
2	98,830.04	9,916.77	96,755.76	10,141.11
3	98,151.65	9,852.47	94,863.33	9,954.79
4	97,402.22	9,781.43	92,764.24	9,748.12

Years 5 through 12 omitted to conserve space.

Yr.	Bal.	Int.	Bal.	Int.
13	85,934.45	8,694.43	59,895.65	6,511.99
14	83,905.72	8,502.13	53,977.78	5,929.34
15	81,664.56	8,289.70	47,413.62	5,283.06
16	79,188.72	8,055.02	40,132.59	4,566.19
17	76,453.63	7,795.77	32,056.41	3,771.04
18	73,432.14	7,509.37	23,098.25	2,889.05
19	70,094.26	7,192.98	13,161.77	1,910.74
20	66,406.86	6,843.46	2,569.05	867.82
21	62,333.34	6,457.34	0.00	34.41
22	57,833.27	6,030.79		
23	52,861.99	5,559.57		
24	47,370.14	5,039.01		
25	41,303.23	4,463.95		
26	34,601.03	3,828.66		
27	27,197.03	3,126.85		
28	19,017.73	2,351.56		
29	9,981.95	1,495.08		
30	0.00	548.91		
		$215,925.77		$139,109.00

> **With this strategy you will never have to make any of these payments!**

Savings With This Strategy:
Interest — $76,816.77   Time — 9 yrs. 11 mos.

Support Information
The Split-Payment Strategy
9.5% Interest Rate
30-Year Comparison

	Reg. Mo. Pmt. Amt. $840.85		Split-Pmt. Amt. $420.43	
Yr.	Bal.	Int.	Bal.	Int.
1	$99,383.36	$9,473.61	$98,441.06	$9,792.60
2	98,705.52	9,412.41	96,720.80	9,631.27
3	97,960.40	9,345.13	94,822.51	9,453.24
4	97,141.33	9,271.18	92,727.78	9,256.80

Years 5 through 12 omitted to conserve space.

Yr.	Bal.	Int.	Bal.	Int.
13	84,953.59	8,170.79	60,874.73	6,269.59
14	82,843.63	7,980.29	55,266.89	5,743.69
15	80,524.26	7,770.88	49,078.71	5,163.35
16	77,974.70	7,540.69	42,250.14	4,522.97
17	75,172.10	7,287.65	34,714.92	3,816.31
18	72,091.35	7,009.50	26,399.90	3,036.52
19	68,704.84	6,703.74	17,224.40	2,176.03
20	64,982.23	6,367.64	7,492.42	1,263.36
21	60,890.16	5,998.18	0.00	<u>269.41</u>
22	56,391.96	5,592.05		
23	51,447.33	5,145.62		
24	46,011.95	4,654.87		
25	40,037.13	4,115.43		
26	33,469.32	3,522.44		
27	26,249.67	2,870.60		
28	18,313.48	2,154.07		
29	9,589.65	1,366.42		
30	0.00	<u>500.60</u>		
		<u>$202,707.51</u>		<u>$134,372.04</u>

> **With this strategy you will never have to make any of these payments!**

Savings With This Strategy:
Interest — $68,335.48   Time — 8 yrs. 6 mos.

Support Information
The Split-Payment Strategy
9% Interest Rate
30-Year Comparison

	Reg. Mo. Pmt. Amt. $804.62		Split-Pmt. Amt. $402.31	
Yr.	Bal.	Int.	Bal.	Int.
1	$99,316.80	$8,972.27	$98,413.51	$9,275.91
2	98,569.52	8,908.19	96,671.87	9,120.77
3	97,752.13	8,838.09	94,759.92	8,950.45
4	96,858.07	8,761.41	92,660.99	8,763.48
Years 5 through 12 omitted to conserve space.				
13	83,919.41	7,651.77	61,660.68	6,001.97
14	81,727.75	7,463.80	56,324.94	5,526.67
15	79,330.49	7,258.21	50,467.41	5,004.88
16	76,708.35	7,033.33	44,037.07	4,432.06
17	73,840.23	6,787.36	36,977.90	3,803.23
18	70,703.07	6,518.31	29,228.40	3,112.91
19	67,271.62	6,224.02	20,721.07	2,355.07
20	63,518.27	5,902.13	11,743.45	1,555.35
21	59,412.84	5,550.04	1,526.25	645.20
22	54,922.28	5,164.92	0.00	12.87
23	50,010.49	4,743.67		
24	44,637.93	4,282.91		
25	38,761.39	3,778.93		
26	32,333.58	3,227.67		
27	25,302.81	2,624.70		
28	17,612.50	1,965.16		
29	9,200.79	1,243.76		
30	0.00	454.68		
		$189,664.14		$129,247.32

> **With this strategy you will never have to make any of these payments!**

Savings With This Strategy:
Interest — $60,416.83   Time — 8 yrs.

Support Information
The Split-Payment Strategy
8.5% Interest Rate
30-Year Comparison

	Reg. Mo. Pmt. Amt. $768.91		Split-Pmt. Amt. $384.46	
Yr.	Bal.	Int.	Bal.	Int.
1	$99,244.04	$8,471.00	$98,378.74	8,759.07
2	98,421.25	8,404.18	96,608.11	8,609.71
3	97,525.75	8,331.45	94,674.37	8,446.59
4	96,551.08	8,252.30	92,562.49	8,268.45

Years 5 through 12 omitted to conserve space.

Yr.	Bal.	Int.	Bal.	Int.
13	82,830.98	7,138.05	62,261.42	5,712.43
14	80,557.44	6,953.41	57,163.49	5,282.40
15	78,082.93	6,752.45	51,595.91	4,812.76
16	75,389.70	6,533.73	45,515.43	4,299.85
17	72,458.41	6,295.67	38,874.78	3,739.68
18	69,268.02	6,036.57	31,622.36	3,127.91
19	65,795.63	5,754.57	23,701.81	2,459.78
20	62,016.31	5,447.64	15,385.74	1,758.29
21	57,902.93	5,113.59	5,969.40	963.99
22	53,425.97	4,750.00	0.00	166.87
23	48,553.29	4,354.28		
24	43,249.91	3,923.58		
25	37,477.75	3,454.81		
26	31,195.39	2,944.60		
27	24,357.73	2,389.30		
28	16,915.68	1,784.91		
29	8,815.82	1,127.10		
30	0.00	411.15		
		$176,808.85		$123,738.78

> **With this strategy you will never have to make any of these payments!**

Savings With This Strategy:
Interest — $53,070.07   Time — 7 yrs. 8 mos.

Support Information
The Split-Payment Strategy
8% Interest Rate
30-Year Comparison

	Reg. Mo. Pmt. Amt. $733.76		Split-Pmt. Amt. $366.88	
Yr.	**Bal.**	**Int.**	**Bal.**	**Int.**
1	$99,164.64	$7,969.81	$98,336.28	$8,242.10
2	98,259.94	7,900.48	96,528.66	8,098.21
3	97,280.15	7,825.39	94,564.71	7,941.87
4	96,219.04	7,744.06	92,430.91	7,772.02
Years 5 through 12 omitted to conserve space.				
13	81,687.61	6,630.40	62,684.55	5,404.14
14	79,332.33	6,449.89	57,793.53	5,014.80
15	76,781.56	6,254.40	52,479.50	4,591.79
16	74,019.08	6,042.69	46,705.88	4,132.20
17	71,027.31	5,813.41	40,432.92	3,632.86
18	67,787.23	5,565.09	33,617.43	3,090.33
19	64,278.22	5,296.17	26,212.49	2,500.88
20	60,477.96	5,004.92	18,477.15	1,885.13
21	56,362.29	4,689.50	9,762.77	1,191.45
22	51,905.02	4,347.90	294.72	437.77
23	47,077.79	3,977.95	0.00	.91
24	41,849.91	3,577.29		
25	36,188.12	3,143.38		
26	30,056.40	2,673.46		
27	23,415.75	2,164.53		
28	16,223.93	1,613.36		
29	8,435.20	1,016.44		
30	0.00	369.98		
		$164,155.25		$117,856.82

> **With this strategy you will never have to make any of these payments!**

Savings With This Strategy:
Interest — $46,298.43   Time — 7 yrs. 2 mos.

Support Information
The Split-Payment Strategy
7.5% Interest Rate
30-Year Comparison

	Reg. Mo. Pmt. Amt. $699.21		Split-Pmt. Amt. $349.61	
Yr.	Bal.	Int.	Bal.	Int.
1	99,078.17	7,468.74	98,285.64	7,725.04
2	98,084.77	7,397.18	96,432.63	7,586.39
3	97,014.25	7,320.06	94,429.76	7,436.52
4	95,860.62	7,236.95	92,264.89	7,274.53

Years 5 through 12 omitted to conserve space.

Yr.	Bal.	Int.	Bal.	Int.
13	80,488.89	6,129.57	62,937.48	5,080.11
14	78,052.35	5,954.04	58,225.62	4,727.54
15	75,426.67	5,764.89	53,132.69	4,346.46
16	72,597.14	5,561.05	47,627.85	3,934.56
17	69,547.95	5,341.38	41,677.81	3,489.35
18	66,262.04	5,104.67	35,246.54	3,008.13
19	62,721.04	4,849.57	28,295.14	2,487.99
20	58,905.15	4,574.68	21,070.35	1,947.39
21	54,793.01	4,278.44	12,972.42	1,341.47
22	50,361.64	3,959.20	4,219.55	686.53
23	45,586.25	3,615.18	0.00	81.50
24	40,440.14	3,244.46		
25	34,894.52	2,844.95		
26	28,918.37	2,414.43		
27	22,478.29	1,950.49		
28	15,538.24	1,450.53		
29	8,059.42	911.75		
30	0.00	331.15		
		$151,717.22		$111,618.16

> **With this strategy you will never have to make any of these payments!**

Savings With This Strategy:
Interest — $40,099.07   Time — 6 yrs. 8 mos.

Support Information
The Split-Payment Strategy
7% Interest Rate
30-Year Comparison

	Reg. Mo. Pmt. Amt. $665.30		Split-Pmt. Amt. $332.65	
Yr.	Bal.	Int.	Bal.	Int.
1	$98,984.19	$6,967.82	$98,226.35	$7,207.93
2	97,894.95	6,894.39	96,319.15	7,074.39
3	96,726.96	6,815.65	94,268.35	6,930.78
4	95,474.55	6,731.21	92,063.14	6,776.37

Years 5 through 12 omitted to conserve space.

Yr.	Bal.	Int.	Bal.	Int.
13	79,234.69	5,636.38	63,027.44	4,743.22
14	76,717.75	5,466.69	58,469.95	4,424.10
15	74,018.87	5,284.74	53,569.32	4,080.95
16	71,124.88	5,089.64	48,299.69	3,711.95
17	68,021.68	4,880.44	42,633.28	3,315.18
18	64,694.16	4,656.11	36,540.23	2,888.53
19	61,126.09	4,415.56	29,988.40	2,429.76
20	57,300.08	4,157.62	23,213.41	1,955.36
21	53,197.49	3,881.04	15,658.15	1,426.32
22	48,798.32	3,584.46	7,534.01	857.45
23	44,081.14	3,266.45	0.00	250.05
24	39,022.95	2,925.44		
25	33,599.10	2,559.78		
26	27,783.17	2,167.69		
27	21,546.80	1,747.26		
28	14,859.60	1,296.43		
29	7,688.98	813.01		
30	0.00	294.65		
		$139,508.90		$105,044.65

With this strategy you will never have to make any of these payments!

Savings With This Strategy:
Interest — $34,464.25   Time — 6 yrs. 3 mos.

7

The Specified Principal-Prepayment Strategy

This strategy is one of those things which sounds absolutely impossible when you first hear of it. By simply adding a **specified amount** to your mortgage payment each month, you can remove one payment from the term of your loan. This strategy allows you to operate your home loan as if it were a high-yield **personal investment program.**

Amortization Schedule Required

For this strategy, **you will definitely need to have an amortization schedule** of your loan. It must be tailor-made to your mortgage to show you the two things you must know to operate this method successfully. You will have to know exactly how much of each payment is being expended for the previous month's interest, and you will need to know exactly how much will be applied to the principal of your loan the following month. If you do not have a personalized amortization schedule, see Chapter 15 for details of how you can obtain one.

Upon examination of your amortization schedule, you will see that the interest cost during **the first two-thirds** of your loan takes **almost the entire amount of each**

monthly payment. Also note that with each payment, the **interest cost goes down** a few cents, and the **principal payment goes up** that same amount. For the greater part of a thirty-year mortgage, the amount that goes toward the principal remains low.

You Must Pay $186,133.12 To Pay Off $7,000.00

If you notice the model mortgage at the end of this chapter, you will see that it takes twelve years and eight months before the lender begins to apply a full $100.00 per month to the principal of your loan. It will take seventeen years and seven months before $200.00 per month is applied against the balance. This is the most discouraging aspect of a thirty-year loan. When you realize that you will pay $180,265.82 on a $100,000.00, 14 1/2% note before a full $100.00 per month begins to be applied to your principal, it is enough to make you sick all over. (See illustration #1 at the end of this chapter.)

Now, pay attention and let the next statement sink in. After paying $180,265.82, you still owe $92,908.76 on the original $100,000.00 that you borrowed. During the first thirteen years of this mortgage it will cost you an unbelievable average of $26,590 for each $1,000 that you pay on the principal balance of this loan.

Don't Get Discouraged

Do not get discouraged. **There is something you should know** about that pitifully small amount which goes against your principal during the first two-thirds of your mortgage. **This is the secret.** If you simply add the amount of next month's principal payment to this month's regular payment, **one whole payment** will automatically be canceled from your loan. That's right! It is canceled **and will never have to be paid!**

Example

Let's use our model thirty-year mortgage of $100,000 at 14.5% interest. The payment is $1,224.56. On the example at the end of this chapter (see illustration #2), you will see that the amount which goes toward interest the first month is $1,208.33. The amount going toward your loan payoff is a **measly** $16.22. Now look just below this figure ($16.22) at the amount that will go toward the principal next month. It is just $16.42. If you add this $16.42 to your regular payment, you will **never have to make payment #2 on your loan!** Increase your first payment by this small amount, and payment #2 can now be skipped. (Do not misunderstand. **You must make a payment every month until the loan is paid in full!**) But the interest amount of that payment is permanently deducted from your mortgage. I say again; **it will never have to be paid.**

Notice that by **investing** only $16.42 in your home mortgage, you have made $1,208.14 in savings on the total cost of your home loan. This is why I call it **a personal investment program.** Every time this is done, the next payment can automatically be skipped and that whole month's interest cost will be saved.

Please note that if you repeat this strategy the following month (payment #3), the added amount should be $16.82, the principal amount of payment #4. Add this amount to payment #3, and the fourth payment will never have to be paid. If you operate this strategy the first two months, you will be saving $2,416.88 in interest as well as taking two months off the length of your mortgage. Your balance will not be the balance of a mortgage that has had two payments made. It will now be the balance of a mortgage that has had four payments made.

Let's Speed It Up

Now let's speed up the process. If you are able to spend just a little more each month, you can really shorten your payoff time. If, when payment #1 is due, you are able to add just $49.86 to your payment, you will be able to skip payments #2, #3, and #4. They will be eliminated by paying their principal amounts. This means that when the second month's payment becomes due, you will make payment #5, not payment #2. What you have done is to make four principal payments at once, bypassing payments #2, #3, and #4. With this move you have saved $3,623.82. That is a great return on only a $49.86 investment. And besides that, you have also **chopped three months off your mortgage.**

Now let's really turn up the heat. Let's say that when payment #1 is due, you have an extra $173.45 to invest. With this amount added to payment #1, you can eliminate payment #2 through payment #11. (See illustration #3 at the end of this chapter.) The interest savings will be a whopping $12,072.15. You have accomplished this with only a $173.45 investment in your mortgage. Very few investments can make you this kind of money.

Now that you know this prepayment secret, you can save a bundle on your mortgage. Why, you might even end up rich!

Support Information
The Specified Principal-Prepayment Strategy
14.5% Interest Rate

Illustration 1
Making One Principal Payment In Advance

Loan Amount	$100,000.00
Term	30 Years
Total Reg. Interest	$340,840.13
Total Reg. Int. & Prin.	$440,840.13

Pmt. Amt.	Prin.	Pmt. No.	Int.	Reg. Bal.
$1,224.56	16.22	1	$1,208.33	$99,983.78
1,224.56	(16.42)*	2	1,208.14	99,967.36**
1,224.56	16.62	3	1,207.94	99,950.74
1,224.56	16.82	4	1,207.74	99,933.92
1,224.56	17.02	5	1,207.53	99,916.90
Payments 6 through 9 omitted to conserve space.				
1,224.56	18.07	10	1,206.48	99,828.66
1,224.56	18.29	11	1,206.26	99,810.37
1,224.56	18.51	12	1,206.04	99,791.86
1,224.56	18.74	13	1,205.82	99,773.12
1,224.56	18.96	14	1,205.59	99,754.15

*Principal Prepayment
**New Balance.

If one principal prepayment is made every month,

Savings With This Strategy:
Interest — $170,119.79   Time — 15 yrs.

Support Information
The Specified Principal-Prepayment Strategy
14.5% Interest Rate

Illustration 2
Making Three Principal Payments In Advance

Loan Amount	$100,000.00
Term	30 Years
Total Reg. Interest	$340,840.13
Total Reg. Int. & Prin.	$440,840.13

Pmt. Amt.	Prin.	Pmt. No.	Int.	Reg. Bal.
$1,224.56	$16.22	1	$1,208.33	$99,983.78
1,224.56	(16.42)*	2	~~1208.14~~	99,967.36
1,224.56	(16.62)*	3	~~1207.94~~	99,950.74
1,224.56	(16.82)*	4	~~1207.74~~	99,933.92**
1,224.56	17.02	5	1207.53	99,916.90
1,224.56	17.23	6	1207.33	99,899.68
1,224.56	17.43	7	1207.12	99,882.24
1,224.56	17.65	8	1206.91	99,864.60
1,224.56	17.86	9	1206.70	99,846.74
1,224.56	18.07	10	1206.48	99,828.66
1,224.56	18.29	11	1206.26	99,810.37
1,224.56	18.51	12	1206.04	99,791.86
1,224.56	18.74	13	1205.82	99,773.12
1,224.56	18.96	14	1205.59	99,754.15

*Principal Prepayments
**New Balance

If three principal prepayments are made every month,

Savings With This Strategy:
Interest — $255,181.51   Time — 21 yrs. 6 mos.

Support Information
The Specified Principal-Prepayment Strategy
14.5% Interest Rate

Illustration 3
Making Ten Principal Payments In Advance

Loan Amount		$100,000.00
Term		30 Years
Total Reg. Interest		$340,840.13
Total Reg. Int. & Prin.		$440,840.13

Pmt. Amt.	Prin.	Pmt. No.	Int.	Reg. Bal.
$1,224.56	16.22	1	$1,208.33	$99,983.78
1,224.56	(16.42)*	~~2~~	~~1,208.14~~	99,967.36
1,224.56	(16.62)*	~~3~~	~~1,207.94~~	99,950.74
1,224.56	(16.82)*	~~4~~	~~1,207.74~~	99,933.92
1,224.56	(17.02)*	~~5~~	~~1,207.53~~	99,916.90
1,224.56	(17.23)*	~~6~~	~~1,207.33~~	99,899.68
1,224.56	(17.43)*	~~7~~	~~1,207.12~~	99,882.24
1,224.56	(17.65)*	~~8~~	~~1,206.91~~	99,864.60
1,224.56	(17.86)*	~~9~~	~~1,206.70~~	99,846.74
1,224.56	(18.07)*	~~10~~	~~1,206.48~~	99,828.66
1,224.56	(18.29)*	~~11~~	~~1,206.26~~	99,810.37**
1,224.56	18.51	12	1,206.04	99,791.86
1,224.56	18.74	13	1,205.82	99,773.12
1,224.56	18.96	14	1,205.59	99,754.15

*Principal Prepayments
**New Balance

If ten principal prepayments are made every month,

Savings With This Strategy:

Interest – $310,113.49   Time – 27 yrs. 3 mos.

8

The Unspecified Principal-Reduction Strategy

This strategy is probably the one with the most possibilities. This is because it has no specified amount which will be prepaid. That amount can be from one cent over the regular payment, all the way to the entire amount of the unpaid balance. It can be a one-time payment, a monthly payment, an annual payment, or any combination of these.

It is impossible to make an amortization chart to fit a paydown schedule which has not yet been decided. However, it is possible to make one for any amount of paydown you might preplan. You may wish to pay down $100 each month beyond your regular payment, or you may wish to make two extra payments per year. You can make payments in lump sums, or they can be paid twice or more yearly. They can be made by adding 1/6, or any portion of a payment to each regular payment. The flexibility of this strategy is unlimited.

If you receive periodic bonuses or tax refunds, they can be added to your regular payment. Every time any extra amount is paid, it will shorten the term of the note. It will also cause an interest cost reduction.

Since the possibilities seem endless, my illustrations will be very limited. I have chosen a few and have displayed them at the end of this chapter.

If you know exactly how much extra you wish to pay each month, an amortization schedule can be drawn to demonstrate the affect it will have on your mortgage. If you do not know exactly how often or how much you will be prepaying, you may wish to have a standard amortization schedule drawn of your mortgage. You could then apply any paydown you wish. All you would have to do is make note of any paydown you make, deducting this amount from that month's principal balance. See Chapter 15 for details of how you can order an amortization schedule with your desired paydown applied, or a standard amortization schedule of your mortgage.

Support Information
The Unspecified Principal-Reduction Strategy
12% Interest Rate

Illustration 1
Making An Additional $100 Principal Payment Each Month

Loan Amount	$100,000.00
Term	30 Years
Payment	$1,028.61
Extra Pymt. Amt.	$100.00

Pmt. No.	Int.	Prin.	Extra Pmt.	Bal.
1	$1,000.00	$28.61	$100.00	$99,871.39
2	998.71	29.90	100.00	99,741.49
3	997.41	31.20	100.00	99,610.29
4	996.10	32.51	100.00	99,477.78
5	994.78	33.83	100.00	99,343.95
6	993.44	35.17	100.00	99,208.77
7	992.09	36.52	100.00	99,072.25
8	990.72	37.89	100.00	98,934.36
9	989.34	39.27	100.00	98,795.09
10	987.95	40.66	100.00	98,654.43
Payments 11 through 212 omitted to conserve space.				
213	57.74	970.87	100.00	4,703.55
214	47.04	981.58	100.00	3,621.97
215	36.22	992.39	100.00	2,529.58
216	25.30	1,003.32	100.00	1,426.26
217	14.26	1,014.35	100.00	311.91
218	3.12	311.91	0.00	0.00

Savings With This Strategy:
Interest — $123,947.96   Time — 11 yrs. 6 mos.

Support Information
The Unspecified Principal-Reduction Strategy
12% Interest Rate

Illustration 2
Making An Additional One-Sixth Principal Payment Each Month

Loan Amount	$100,000.00
Term	30 Years
Payment	$1,028.61
Extra Pymt. Amt.	$171.44

Pmt. No.	Int.	Prin.	Extra Pmt.	Bal.
1	$1,000.00	$28.61	$171.44	$99,799.95
2	998.00	30.61	171.44	99,597.89
3	995.98	32.63	171.44	99,393.82
4	993.94	34.67	171.44	99,187.71
5	991.88	36.74	171.44	98,979.53
6	989.80	38.82	171.44	98,769.27
7	987.69	40.92	171.44	98,556.91
8	985.57	43.04	171.44	98,342.43
9	983.42	45.19	171.44	98,125.80
10	981.26	47.35	171.44	97,907.01
Payments 11 through 174 omitted to conserve space.				
175	58.79	969.82	171.44	4,738.00
176	47.38	981.23	171.44	3,585.32
177	35.85	992.76	171.44	2,421.13
178	24.21	1,004.40	171.44	1,245.28
179	12.45	1,016.16	171.44	57.68
180	.58	57.68	0.00	0.00

Savings With This Strategy:
Interest — $154,232.80   Time — 15 yrs.

Support Information
The Unspecified Principal-Reduction Strategy
11.5% Interest Rate

Illustration 1
Making An Additional $100 Principal Payment Each Month

Loan Amount	$100,000.00
Term	30 Years
Payment	$990.29
Extra Pymt. Amt.	$100.00

Pmt. No.	Int.	Prin.	Extra Pmt.	Bal.
1	$958.33	$31.96	$100.00	$99,868.04
2	957.07	33.22	100.00	99,734.82
3	955.79	34.50	100.00	99,600.32
4	954.50	35.79	100.00	99,464.53
5	953.20	37.09	100.00	99,327.44
6	951.89	38.40	100.00	99,189.04
7	950.56	39.73	100.00	99,049.31
8	949.22	41.07	100.00	98,908.24
9	947.87	42.42	100.00	98,765.82
10	946.51	43.79	100.00	98,622.03
Payments 11 through 215 omitted to conserve space.				
216	54.80	935.49	100.00	4,683.07
217	44.88	945.41	100.00	3,637.66
218	34.86	955.43	100.00	2,582.23
219	24.75	965.55	100.00	1,516.69
220	14.53	975.76	100.00	440.93
221	4.23	440.93	0.00	0.00

Savings With This Strategy:
Interest — $115,105.36   Time — 11 yrs. 7 mos.

Support Information
The Unspecified Principal-Reduction Strategy
11.5% Interest Rate

Illustration 2
Making An Additional One-Sixth Principal Payment Each Month

Loan Amount	$100,000.00
Term	30 Years
Payment	$990.29
Extra Pymt. Amt.	$165.04

Pmt. No.	Int.	Prin.	Extra Pmt.	Bal.
1	$958.33	$31.96	$165.04	$99,803.00
2	956.45	33.85	165.04	99,604.12
3	954.54	35.75	165.04	99,403.32
4	952.62	37.68	165.04	99,200.61
5	950.67	39.62	165.04	98,995.95
6	948.71	41.58	165.04	98,789.33
7	946.73	43.56	165.04	98,580.73
8	944.73	45.56	165.04	98,370.13
9	942.71	47.58	165.04	98,157.51
10	940.68	49.62	165.04	97,942.86
Payments 11 through 179 omitted to conserve space.				
180	58.72	931.57	165.04	5,030.61
181	48.21	942.08	165.04	3,923.49
182	37.60	952.69	165.04	2,805.76
183	26.89	963.40	165.04	1,677.32
184	16.07	974.22	165.04	538.06
185	5.16	538.06	0.00	0.00

Savings With This Strategy:
Interest — $142,225.39   Time — 14 yrs. 7 mos.

Support Information
The Unspecified Principal-Reduction Strategy
11% Interest Rate

Illustration 1
Making An Additional $100 Principal Payment Each Month

Loan Amount	$100,000.00
Term	30 Years
Payment	$952.32
Extra Pymt. Amt.	$100.00

Pmt. No.	Int.	Prin.	Extra Pmt.	Bal.
1	$916.67	$35.66	$100.00	$99,864.34
2	915.42	36.90	100.00	99,727.44
3	914.17	38.16	100.00	99,589.29
4	912.90	39.42	100.00	99,449.87
5	911.62	40.70	100.00	99,309.17
6	910.33	41.99	100.00	99,167.18
7	909.03	43.29	100.00	99,023.89
8	907.72	44.60	100.00	98,879.28
9	906.39	45.93	100.00	98,733.35
10	905.06	47.27	100.00	98,586.08
Payments 11 through 218 omitted to conserve space.				
219	51.60	900.73	100.00	4,627.92
220	42.42	909.90	100.00	3,618.02
221	33.17	919.16	100.00	2,598.86
222	23.82	928.50	100.00	1,570.36
223	14.40	937.93	100.00	532.44
224	4.88	532.44	0.00	0.00

Savings With This Strategy:

Interest — $106,578.66   Time — 11 yrs. 3 mos.

Support Information
The Unspecified Principal-Reduction Strategy
11% Interest Rate

Illustration 2
Making An Additional One-Sixth Principal Payment Each Month

Loan Amount	$100,000.00
Term	30 Years
Payment	$952.32
Extra Pymt. Amt.	$158.72

Pmt. No.	Int.	Prin.	Extra Pmt.	Bal.
1	$916.67	$35.66	$158.72	$99,805.62
2	914.88	37.44	158.72	99,609.46
3	913.09	39.24	158.72	99,411.51
4	911.27	41.05	158.72	99,211.74
5	909.44	42.88	158.72	99,010.13
6	907.59	44.73	158.72	98,806.68
7	905.73	46.60	158.72	98,601.37
8	903.85	48.48	158.72	98,394.17
9	901.95	50.38	158.72	98,185.07
10	900.03	52.29	158.72	97,974.06
Payments 11 through 185 omitted to conserve space.				
186	49.98	902.35	158.72	4,390.82
187	40.25	912.07	158.72	3,320.02
188	30.43	921.89	158.72	2,239.41
189	20.53	931.80	158.72	1,148.90
190	10.53	941.79	158.72	48.39
191	0.44	48.39	0.00	0.00

Savings With This Strategy:
Interest — $130,578.30   Time — 14 yrs. 1 mo.

Support Information
The Unspecified Principal-Reduction Strategy
10.5% Interest Rate

Illustration 1
Making An Additional $100 Principal Payment Each Month

Loan Amount	$100,000.00
Term	30 Years
Payment	$914.74
Extra Pymt. Amt.	$100.00

Pmt. No.	Int.	Prin.	Extra Pmt.	Bal.
1	$875.00	$39.74	$100.00	$99,860.26
2	873.78	40.96	100.00	99,719.30
3	872.54	42.20	100.00	99,577.10
4	871.30	43.44	100.00	99,433.66
5	870.04	44.69	100.00	99,288.97
6	868.78	45.96	100.00	99,143.01
7	867.50	47.24	100.00	98,995.77
8	866.21	48.53	100.00	98,847.24
9	864.91	49.83	100.00	98,697.42
10	863.60	51.14	100.00	98,546.28
Payments 11 through 221 omitted to conserve space.				
222	48.10	866.64	100.00	4,530.07
223	39.64	875.10	100.00	3,554.97
224	31.11	883.63	100.00	2,571.33
225	22.50	892.24	100.00	1,579.09
226	13.82	900.92	100.00	578.17
227	5.06	578.17	0.00	0.00

Savings With This Strategy:
Interest — $98,377.10   Time — 11 yrs.

Support Information
The Unspecified Principal-Reduction Strategy
10.5% Interest Rate

Illustration 2
Making An Additional One-Sixth Principal Payment Each Month

Loan Amount		$100,000.00
Term		30 Years
Payment		$914.74
Extra Pymt. Amt.		$152.45

Pmt. No.	Int.	Prin.	Extra Pmt.	Bal.
1	$875.00	$39.74	$152.45	$99,807.81
2	873.32	41.42	152.45	99,613.94
3	871.62	43.12	152.45	99,418.37
4	869.91	44.83	152.45	99,221.09
5	868.18	46.55	152.45	99,022.09
6	866.44	48.30	152.45	98,821.34
7	864.69	50.05	152.45	98,618.84
8	862.91	51.82	152.45	98,414.57
9	861.13	53.61	152.45	98,208.50
10	859.32	55.41	152.45	98,000.64
Payments 11 through 190 omitted to conserve space.				
191	52.37	862.36	152.45	4,970.84
192	43.49	871.24	152.45	3,947.14
193	34.54	880.20	152.45	2,914.49
194	25.50	889.24	152.45	1,872.80
195	16.39	898.35	152.45	822.00
196	7.19	822.00	0.00	0.00

Savings With This Strategy:
Interest — $119,307.85   Time — 13 yrs. 8 mos.

Support Information
The Unspecified Principal-Reduction Strategy
10% Interest Rate

Illustration 1
Making An Additional $100 Principal Payment Each Month

Loan Amount	$100,000.00
Term	30 Years
Payment	$877.57
Extra Pymt. Amt.	$100.00

Pmt. No.	Int.	Prin.	Extra Pmt.	Bal.
1	$833.33	$44.24	$100.00	$99,855.76
2	832.13	45.44	100.00	99,710.32
3	830.92	46.65	100.00	99,563.67
4	829.70	47.87	100.00	99,415.79
5	828.46	49.11	100.00	99,266.69
6	827.22	50.35	100.00	99,116.34
7	825.97	51.60	100.00	98,964.74
8	824.71	52.87	100.00	98,811.87
9	823.43	54.14	100.00	98,657.73
10	822.15	55.42	100.00	98,502.31
Payments 11 through 224 omitted to conserve space.				
225	44.30	833.27	100.00	4,382.64
226	36.52	841.05	100.00	3,441.59
227	28.68	848.89	100.00	2,492.70
228	20.77	856.80	100.00	1,535.90
229	12.80	864.77	100.00	571.13
230	4.76	571.13	0.00	0.00

Savings With This Strategy:
Interest — $90,508.42   Time — 12 yrs. 9 mos.

Support Information
The Unspecified Principal-Reduction Strategy
10% Interest Rate

Illustration 2
Making An Additional One-Sixth Principal Payment Each Month

Loan Amount	$100,000.00	
Term	30 Years	
Payment	$877.57	
Extra Pymt. Amt.	$146.26	

Pmt. No.	Int.	Prin.	Extra Pmt.	Bal.
1	$833.33	$44.24	$146.26	$99,809.50
2	831.75	45.83	146.26	99,617.42
3	830.15	47.43	146.26	99,423.73
4	828.53	49.04	146.26	99,228.43
5	826.90	50.67	146.26	99,031.50
6	825.26	52.31	146.26	98,832.93
7	823.61	53.96	146.26	98,632.71
8	821.94	55.63	146.26	98,430.82
9	820.26	57.31	146.26	98,227.24
10	818.56	59.01	146.26	98,021.97
11	816.85	60.72	146.26	97,814.99
12	815.12	62.45	146.26	97,606.28

Payments 13 through 198 omitted to conserve space.

199	30.46	847.11	146.26	2,661.84
200	22.18	855.39	146.26	1,660.19
201	13.83	863.74	146.26	650.19
202	5.42	650.19	0.00	0.00

Savings With This Strategy:
Interest — 108,456.18   Time — 13 yrs. 2 mos.

Support Information
The Unspecified Principal-Reduction Strategy
9.5% Interest Rate

<u>Illustration 1</u>
Making An Additional $100 Principal Payment Each Month

Loan Amount	$100,000.00
Term	30 Years
Payment	$840.85
Extra Pymt. Amt.	$100.00

Pmt. No.	Int.	Prin.	Extra Pmt.	Bal.
1	$791.67	$49.19	$100.00	$99,850.81
2	790.49	50.37	100.00	99,700.44
3	789.30	51.56	100.00	99,548.88
4	788.10	52.76	100.00	99,396.13
5	786.89	53.97	100.00	99,242.16
6	785.67	55.19	100.00	99,086.97
7	784.44	56.42	100.00	98,930.55
8	783.20	57.65	100.00	98,772.90
9	781.95	58.90	100.00	98,614.00
10	780.69	60.16	100.00	98,453.84
Payments 11 through 227 omitted to conserve space.				
228	40.22	800.63	100.00	4,180.05
229	33.09	807.76	100.00	3,272.29
230	25.91	814.95	100.00	2,357.34
231	18.66	822.19	100.00	1,435.15
232	11.36	829.49	100.00	505.66
233	4.00	505.66	0.00	0.00

Savings With This Strategy:
Interest — $82,978.82   Time — 10 yrs. 6 mos.

Support Information
The Unspecified Principal-Reduction Strategy
9.5% Interest Rate

Illustration 2
Making An Additional One-Sixth Principal Payment Each Month

Loan Amount	$100,000.00
Term	30 Years
Payment	$840.85
Extra Pymt. Amt.	$140.14

Pmt. No.	Int.	Prin.	Extra Pmt.	Bal.
1	$791.67	$49.19	$140.14	$99,810.67
2	790.17	50.69	140.14	99,619.85
3	788.66	52.20	140.14	99,427.51
4	787.13	53.72	140.14	99,233.65
5	785.60	55.25	140.14	99,038.25
6	784.05	56.80	140.14	98,841.31
7	782.49	58.36	140.14	98,642.81
8	780.92	59.93	140.14	98,442.74
9	779.34	61.52	140.14	98,241.09
10	777.74	63.11	140.14	98,037.83
Payments 11 through 202 omitted to conserve space.				
203	42.54	798.31	140.14	4,435.04
204	35.11	805.74	140.14	3,489.16
205	27.62	813.23	140.14	2,535.79
206	20.07	820.78	140.14	1,574.87
207	12.47	828.39	140.14	606.34
208	4.80	606.34	0.00	0.00

Savings With This Strategy:
Interest — $93,815.71   Time — 12 yr. 8 mos.

Support Information
The Unspecified Principal-Reduction Strategy
9% Interest Rate

Illustration 1
Making An Additional $100 Principal Payment Each Month

Loan Amount	$100,000.00
Term	30 Years
Payment	$804.62
Extra Pymt. Amt.	$100.00

Pmt. No.	Int.	Prin.	Extra Pmt.	Bal.
1	$750.00	$54.62	$100.00	$99,845.38
2	748.84	55.78	100.00	99,689.60
3	747.67	56.95	100.00	99,532.64
4	746.49	58.13	100.00	99,374.52
5	745.31	59.31	100.00	99,215.20
6	744.11	60.51	100.00	99,054.69
7	742.91	61.71	100.00	98,892.98
8	741.70	62.93	100.00	98,730.06
9	740.48	64.15	100.00	98,565.91
10	739.24	65.38	100.00	98,400.53
Payments 11 through 230 omitted to conserve space.				
231	35.90	768.72	100.00	3,918.06
232	29.39	775.24	100.00	3,042.83
233	22.82	781.80	100.00	2,161.03
234	16.21	788.41	100.00	1,272.61
235	9.54	795.08	100.00	377.53
236	2.83	377.53	0.00	0.00

Savings With This Strategy:
Interest — $75,792.84   Time — 10 yrs. 3 mos.

Support Information
The Unspecified Principal-Reduction Strategy
9% Interest Rate

Illustration 2
Making An Additional One-Sixth Principal Payment Each Month

Loan Amount	$100,000.00
Term	30 Years
Payment	$804.62
Extra Pymt. Amt.	$134.10

Pmt. No.	Int.	Prin.	Extra Pmt.	Bal.
1	$750.00	$54.62	$134.10	$99,811.28
2	748.58	56.04	134.10	99,621.14
3	747.16	57.46	134.10	99,429.58
4	745.72	58.90	134.10	99,236.57
5	744.27	60.35	134.10	99,042.13
6	742.82	61.81	134.10	98,846.22
7	741.35	63.28	134.10	98,648.84
8	739.87	64.76	134.10	98,449.99
9	738.37	66.25	134.10	98,249.64
10	736.87	67.75	134.10	98,047.79
Payments 11 through 208 omitted to conserve space.				
209	39.14	765.48	134.10	4,319.26
210	32.39	772.23	134.10	3,412.94
211	25.60	779.03	134.10	2,499.81
212	18.75	785.87	134.10	1,579.84
213	11.85	792.77	134.10	652.96
214	4.90	652.96	0.00	0.00

Savings With This Strategy:
Interest — $84,261.69   Time — 12 yrs. 2 mos.

Support Information
The Unspecified Principal-Reduction Strategy
8.5% Interest Rate

Illustration 1
Making An Additional $100 Principal Payment Each Month

Loan Amount	$100,000.00
Term	30 Years
Payment	$768.91
Extra Pymt. Amt.	$100.00

Pmt. No.	Int.	Prin.	Extra Pmt.	Bal.
1	$708.33	$60.58	$100.00	$99,839.42
2	707.20	61.72	100.00	99,677.70
3	706.05	62.86	100.00	99,514.84
4	704.90	64.02	100.00	99,350.82
5	703.73	65.18	100.00	99,185.64
6	702.56	66.35	100.00	99,019.30
7	701.39	67.53	100.00	98,851.77
8	700.20	68.71	100.00	98,683.06
9	699.00	69.91	100.00	98,513.15
10	697.80	71.11	100.00	98,342.03
Payments 11 through 233 omitted to conserve space.				
234	31.39	737.52	100.00	3,593.87
235	25.46	743.46	100.00	2,750.41
236	19.48	749.43	100.00	1,900.98
237	13.47	755.45	100.00	1,045.53
238	7.41	761.51	100.00	184.02
239	1.30	184.02	0.00	0.00

Savings With This Strategy:
Interest — $68,953.20   Time — 10 yrs. 1 mo.

Support Information
The Unspecified Principal-Reduction Strategy
8.5% Interest Rate

Illustration 2
Making An Additional One-Sixth Principal Payment Each Month

Loan Amount	$100,000.00
Term	30 Years
Payment	$768.91
Extra Pymt. Amt.	$128.15

Pmt. No.	Int.	Prin.	Extra Pmt.	Bal.
1	$708.33	$60.58	$128.15	$99,811.27
2	707.00	61.92	128.15	99,621.20
3	705.65	63.26	128.15	99,429.79
4	704.29	64.62	128.15	99,237.02
5	702.93	65.98	128.15	99,042.89
6	701.55	67.36	128.15	98,847.38
7	700.17	68.74	128.15	98,650.48
8	698.77	70.14	128.15	98,452.19
9	697.37	71.54	128.15	98,252.50
10	695.96	72.96	128.15	98,051.39
Payments 11 through 214 omitted to conserve space.				
215	36.26	732.65	128.15	4,258.22
216	30.16	738.75	128.15	3,391.31
217	24.02	744.89	128.15	2,518.27
218	17.84	751.08	128.15	1,639.05
219	11.61	757.30	128.15	753.59
220	5.34	753.59	0.00	0.00

Savings With This Strategy:
Interest — $75,196.07   Time — 11 yrs. 8 mos.

Support Information
The Unspecified Principal-Reduction Strategy
8% Interest Rate

Illustration 1
Making An Additional $100 Principal Payment Each Month

Loan Amount	$100,000.00
Term	30 Years
Payment	$733.76
Extra Pymt. Amt.	$100.00

Pmt. No.	Int.	Prin.	Extra Pmt.	Bal.
1	$666.67	$67.10	$100.00	$99,832.90
2	665.55	68.21	100.00	99,664.69
3	664.43	69.33	100.00	99,495.36
4	663.30	70.46	100.00	99,324.89
5	662.17	71.60	100.00	99,153.30
6	661.02	72.74	100.00	98,980.55
7	659.87	73.89	100.00	98,806.66
8	666.67	67.10	100.00	99,832.90
9	665.55	68.21	100.00	99,664.69
10	664.43	69.33	100.00	99,495.36
Payments 11 through 235 omitted to conserve space.				
236	32.10	701.67	100.00	4,013.13
237	26.75	707.01	100.00	3,206.12
238	21.37	712.39	100.00	2,393.73
239	15.96	717.81	100.00	1,575.92
240	10.51	723.26	100.00	752.66
241	5.02	728.75	23.92	0.00

Savings With This Strategy:
Interest — $62,460.31   Time — 9 yrs. 10 mos.

Support Information
The Unspecified Principal-Reduction Strategy
8% Interest Rate

Illustration 2
Making An Additional One-Sixth Principal Payment Each Month

Loan Amount	$100,000.00
Term	30 Years
Payment	$733.76
Extra Pymt. Amt.	$122.29

Pmt. No.	Int.	Prin.	Extra Pmt.	Bal.
1	$666.67	$67.10	$122.29	$99,810.61
2	665.40	68.36	122.29	99,619.96
3	664.13	69.63	122.29	99,428.04
4	662.85	70.91	122.29	99,234.84
5	661.57	72.20	122.29	99,040.35
6	660.27	73.50	122.29	98,844.56
7	658.96	74.80	122.29	98,647.47
8	657.65	76.11	122.29	98,449.07
9	656.33	77.44	122.29	98,249.34
10	655.00	78.77	122.29	98,048.28
Payments 11 through 221 omitted to conserve space.				
222	28.16	705.60	122.29	3,396.11
223	22.64	711.12	122.29	2,562.69
224	17.08	716.68	122.29	1,723.72
225	11.49	722.27	122.29	879.16
226	5.86	727.90	122.29	28.97
227	0.19	28.97	0.00	0.00

Savings With This Strategy:
Interest — $66,641.99   Time — 11 yrs. 1 mo.

9

The Planned-Increase Payment Strategy

Once you have conquered impulse spending, you will be able to budget your income and outgo. When this time has come, you will have the necessary funds to perform some more exotic mortgage payment strategies.

The planned-increase payment strategy **is not for the financially undisciplined.** It will only bring them disappointment. However, if you can discipline yourself to make a systematic percentage of increase in your house payment each year, you can quickly **take the rule over your home loan.**

Example

Let's once again use our thirty-year, $100,000 mortgage at 14.5% interest as an example. To operate this strategy, you must increase the house payment of $1,224.56 per month just one percent per year beginning with the first payment. This means that instead of paying $1,224.56, you will make payments of $1,236.81 for the first twelve months. Then you must increase the payment by one percent each year thereafter. This will increase your payment to $1,249.18 for the second twelve months of your loan. Each year you should budget your income to enable you to add another one percent to the previous year's payment. If this is faithfully done every year, you will find that after only twelve years, the entire loan will be paid in full.

Notice that this strategy will pay off the loan in only 144 payments instead of the normal 360 payments (thirty years). It will also save you $151,778.84 in interest.

This strategy works even faster when an annual increase of more than one percent is planned. The illustration at the end of this chapter will show you what happens to a $100,000.00 mortgage at a 12% interest rate when yearly increases from one to ten percent are used.

Varying Increases

This same strategy can also be accomplished with varying percentages of increase, such as one percent the first year, two percent the second year, three percent the third year, and so on. This is also illustrated at the end of this chapter.

It would be impossible to illustrate all the many possibilities this method allows. If you have a specific plan of increase in mind that you would like to see applied to your own mortgage, see Chapter 15 for details of how you can obtain an amortization schedule which applies this plan to your loan.

Support Information

The Planned-Increase Payment Strategy

12% Interest Rate

Illustration 1

Increasing The Payment One Percent Per Year

Loan Amt. — $100,000.00   Total Int. — $111,530.29   Pmt. — $1,028.61

Yr.	%	RegPymt.+%	AnnPymt.+%	Prin.	Int.	Bal.
1	1%	$1,038.90	$12,466.78	$493.33	$11,973.45	$99,506.67
2	2%	1,059.68	12,716.12	819.42	11,896.70	98,687.25
3	3%	1,091.47	13,097.60	1,326.52	11,771.08	97,360.73
4	4%	1,135.13	13,621.51	2,048.46	11,573.05	95,312.27
5	5%	1,191.88	14,302.58	3,028.06	11,274.52	92,284.21
6	6%	1,263.39	15,160.74	4,319.06	10,841.68	87,965.15
7	7%	1,351.83	16,221.99	5,988.44	10,233.55	81,976.71
			Payments 8 through 9 omitted to conserve space.			
10	10%	1,750.51	21,006.18	14,205.67	6,800.51	48,835.84
11	10%	1,925.57	23,106.80	18,227.40	4,879.40	30,608.45
12	10%	2,118.12	25,417.48	22,981.19	2,436.29	7,627.26
13	10%	2,329.94	7,796.25	7,627.26	168.96	0.00

Savings With The Planned-Increase Strategy

Interest — $158,770.24   Time — 17 yrs. 6 mos.

Support Information
The Planned-Increase Payment Strategy
12% Interest
Illustration 2

Increasing The Payment Two Percent Per Year

Loan Amt. — $100,000.00   Total Int. — $89,237.45   Pmt. — $1,028.61

Yr.	%	RegPmt.+%	AnnPmt.+%	Prin.	Int.	Bal.
1	2%	$1,049.18	$12,590.22	623.79	11,966.43	99,376.21
2	4%	1,091.15	13,093.83	1,235.15	11,858.68	98,141.06
3	6%	1,156.62	13,879.46	2,222.11	11,657.35	95,918.95
4	8%	1,249.15	14,989.81	3,677.44	11,312.37	92,241.51
5	10%	1,374.07	16,488.79	5,728.07	10,760.73	86,513.45
6	12%	1,538.95	18,467.45	8,545.72	9,921.73	77,967.73
7	14%	1,754.41	21,052.89	12,362.02	8,690.87	65,605.71
8	14%	2,000.02	24,000.30	17,044.87	6,955.42	48,560.83
9	14%	2,280.03	27,360.34	22,757.74	4,602.60	25,803.09
10	14%	2,599.23	27,314.36	25,803.09	1,511.27	0.00

Savings With This Strategy
Interest — $181,063.09   Time — 20 yrs.

Support Information

The Planned-Increase Payment Strategy

12% Interest

Illustration 3

Increasing The Payment From Five To Ten Percent

Yr.	%	RegPmt.+%	AnnPmt.+%	Prin.	Int.	Bal.
		Loan Amt. — $100,000.00	Total Int. — $84,974.04		Pmt. — $1,028.61	
1	5%	$1,080.04	$12,960.52	1,015.15	11,945.37	98,984.85
2	6%	1,144.85	13,738.15	1,965.75	11,772.40	97,019.10
3	7%	1,224.99	14,699.82	3,231.43	11,468.39	93,787.67
4	8%	1,322.98	15,875.81	4,884.12	10,991.68	88,903.55
5	9%	1,442.05	17,304.63	7,013.64	10,290.99	81,889.91
6	10%	1,586.26	19,035.09	9,732.03	9,303.06	72,157.88
7	10%	1,744.88	20,938.60	12,978.06	7,960.54	59,179.82
8	10%	1,919.37	23,032.46	16,836.95	6,195.51	42,342.87
9	10%	2,111.31	25,335.71	21,406.55	3,929.16	20,936.32
10	10%	2,322.44	22,053.26	20,936.32	1,116.94	0.00

Savings With This Strategy:

Interest — $185,326.49   Time — 20 yrs. 2 mos.

Support Information

The Planned-Increase Payment Strategy

12% Interest

Illustration 4

Increasing The Payment From Ten Percent To Fourteen Percent

Loan Amt. — $100,000.00   Total Int. — $67,089.57   Pmt. — $1,028.61

Yr.	%	RegPmt.+%	AnnPmt.+%	Prin.	Int.	Bal.
1	10%	$1,131.47	$13,577.69	1,667.42	11,910.27	98,332.58
2	11%	1,255.94	15,071.23	3,457.38	11,613.85	94,875.20
3	12%	1,406.65	16,879.78	5,807.27	11,072.51	89,067.93
4	13%	1,589.51	19,074.15	8,862.95	10,211.20	80,204.98
5	14%	1,812.04	21,744.53	12,809.26	8,935.27	67,395.72
6	14%	2,065.73	24,788.77	17,651.17	7,137.60	49,744.55
7	14%	2,354.93	28,259.19	23,557.59	4,701.61	26,186.96
8	14%	2,684.62	27,694.22	26,186.96	1,507.26	0.00

Savings With This Strategy:

Interest — $203,210.97   Time — 22 yrs. 1 mo.

10

The Shorter-Term Strategy

The strategy I am suggesting in this chapter does not apply to existing mortgages. It is for those people who are about to sign a new mortgage. Before you sign a loan of any kind, you should be made aware of all the **time options** available to you.

Ignorance Rules

It seems as if most people do not know they can borrow money on a house **for less than thirty years.** This is evident when you see the disproportionate number of thirty-year loans made by home buyers. I draw this information from personal experience as well as from statistics.

In my early years I was in the home building business in Florida. A great deal of my time was spent in new home sales. As I would help our customers make arrangements for their financing, **almost no one ever asked me about any shorter term for a loan.** They just settled for a thirty-year loan without even inquiring about how much a shorter-term loan would cost per month.

Lower Interest

A little known advantage of purchasing your home on a shorter term is that many times the bank will **lower your interest rate.** This can amount to as much as one full percentage point or more. The interest rate reduction will vary according to how short a term you are willing to take to repay the loan.

The reason lenders may consider lowering the interest rate on a shorter term loan is obvious. They are locked in to that interest rate for a shorter period of time.

Five-Year Increments

Shortening the term of a mortgage is usually done in increments of five years. So our illustration will take our standard thirty-year, $100,000 mortgage at 14.5% interest, indicating the extra amount you would have to pay to reduce the term to twenty-five years, and all the way down to five years. This will also be illustrated with various interest rates.

For instance, if you notice the chart at the end of this chapter, you will see that if you wish to decrease the term of a 14.5% mortgage to twenty-five years, you only have to add $17.60 to your payment. If you wish to pay this mortgage off in twenty years, you would only have to pay $55.44 more. At fifteen years, the added payment would be $140.94. If you want to pay off your house in just ten years, you would have to add $324.56. It is possible that you could even pay off the whole house in only five years.

To do so, it would take less than twice the payment to cut twenty-five years off your mortgage.

Isn't it surprising how little per month extra it costs to take large periods of time off a thirty-year mortgage?

Support Information
The Shorter-Term Strategy

Loan Amount $100,000.00

		Number of Years			
Int.	**30**	**25**	**20**	**15**	**10**	**5**
14.5%	1224.56	1242.16	1280.00	1365.50	1582.87	2352.03
14.0%	1184.87	1203.76	1243.52	1331.74	1552.66	2326.83
13.5%	1145.41	1165.64	1207.37	1298.32	1522.66	2300.98
13.0%	1106.20	1127.84	1171.58	1265.24	1493.11	2275.31
12.5%	1067.26	1090.35	1136.14	1223.52	1463.76	2249.79
12.0%	1028.61	1053.22	1101.09	1200.17	1434.71	2224.44
11.5%	990.29	1016.47	1066.43	1168.19	1405.95	2199.26
11.0%	952.32	980.11	1032.19	1136.60	1377.50	2174.24
10.5%	914.74	944.18	998.38	1105.40	1349.35	2149.39
10.0%	877.57	908.70	965.02	1074.61	1321.51	2124.70
9.5%	840.85	873.70	932.13	1044.22	1293.98	2100.19
9.0%	804.62	839.20	899.73	1014.27	1266.76	2075.84
8.5%	768.91	805.23	867.82	984.74	1239.86	2051.65
8.0%	733.76	771.82	836.44	955.65	1213.28	2027.64

This illustration shows the payment needed to reduce the term of the mortgage to the desired number of years.

11

The Targeted-Date Strategy

Since every person's personal plans differ, it is impossible to say exactly what mortgage term each individual needs. Of course, everyone would like to have his mortgage paid in full tomorrow. Unfortunately this is not always possible. However, most people know of upcoming situations which will drastically affect their income.

Retirement

Knowing how to shift the payoff date of your mortgage can be of great help. For instance, you may be retiring in **twelve years** but still have **twenty years** of payments remaining on your mortgage. This strategy can determine the additional amount you would have to add to your regular monthly payment to see your mortgage paid in full on the day you retire. This would be especially helpful in offsetting the drop in income that usually accompanies retirement.

College Tuition

Another instance where this strategy can be very helpful is when a family is faced with the expense of college tuition. If the parents took out a thirty-year mortgage four years before their child was born, they know they will still owe approximately nine years of payments by the time their child begins college. By adding a predetermined amount to each monthly payment, they can have the mortgage paid off the day tuition costs begin. This will free the entire amount of the house payment to finance their child's education.

Following are illustrations using the $100,000 thirty-year mortgage from 15% interest through 7% interest, with several time-targeted reductions. You will see exactly how much must be added to each payment to reduce the mortgage by specific periods of time.

The only accurate way to accomplish this strategy for your targeted payoff date is to have a tailor-made amortization schedule applying this plan to the desired date of payoff. See Chapter 15 for details of how to obtain this special schedule.

Support Information
The Targeted-Date Strategy

15% Interest Rate

Yrs. to Save	Reg. Pmt.	Added Pmt.	Total Pmt.	Int. Saved.
1	$1,264.45	$2.50	$1,266.95	$15,169.04
2		5.20	1,269.65	29,122.42
7		27.75	1,292.20	99,230.50
10		53.00	1,317.45	139,960.02
12		78.00	1,342.45	166,017.77
15		136.00	1,400.45	203,654.97

14.5% Interest

Yrs. to Save	Reg. Pmt.	Added Pmt.	Total Pmt.	Int. Saved.
1	$1,224.56	$2.75	$1,227.31	$14,779.54
2		5.60	1,230.16	27,882.56
7		29.50	1,254.06	95,006.37
10		56.00	1,280.56	134,267.77
12		82.00	1,306.56	159,303.67
15		142.00	1,366.56	245,306.89

13% Interest

Yrs. to Save	Reg. Pmt.	Added Pmt.	Total Pmt.	Int. Saved.
1	$1,106.20	$3.25	$1,109.45	$12,212.14
2		7.00	1,113.20	24,420.73
7		36.00	1,142.20	83,881.93
10		66.50	1,172.70	117,610.22
12		161.00	1,267.20	139,427.68
15		142.00	1,248.20	171,211.63

Support Information
The Targeted-Date Strategy
Continued

12% Interest

Yrs. to Save	Reg. Pmt.	Added Pmt.	Total Pmt.	Int. Saved.
1	$1,028.61	$3.75	$1,032.36	$11,048.62
2		8.00	1,036.61	21,993.86
7		40.00	1,068.61	75,420.54
10		73.00	1,101.61	106,418.22
12		104.00	1,132.61	126,140.28
15		122.00	1,150.61	154,393.13

11% Interest

Yrs. to Save	Reg. Pmt.	Added Pmt.	Total Pmt.	Int. Saved.
1	$952.32	$4.55	$956.87	$10,453.93
2		9.25	961.57	19,953.52
7		45.00	997.32	67,958.52
10		80.00	1,032.32	95,183.87
12		113.00	1,065.32	112,898.83
15		185.00	1,137.32	138,435.06

10% Interest

Yrs. to Save	Reg. Pmt.	Added Pmt.	Total Pmt.	Int. Saved.
1	$877.57	$5.00	$882.57	$8,980.77
2		10.50	888.07	17,733.22
7		50.00	927.57	60,321.86
10			965.57	84,593.90
12		123.00	1,000.57	100,226.25
15		199.00	1,076.57	122,943.53

Support Information
The Targeted-Date Strategy
Continued

9% Interest

Yrs. to Save	Reg. Pmt.	Added Pmt.	Total Pmt.	Int. Saved.
1	$804.62	$6.00	$810.62	$8,339.60
2		12.00	816.62	15,763.63
7		55.00	859.62	52,724.09
10		96.00	900.62	74,106.25
12		133.00	937.62	87,761.09
15		210.00	1,014.62	107,495.99

8% Interest

Yrs. to Save	Reg. Pmt.	Added Pmt.	Total Pmt.	Int. Saved.
1	$733.76	$6.25	$740.01	$7,642.20
2		13.00	746.76	13,284.86
7		60.00	793.76	45,319.08
10		103.00	836.76	63,518.88
12		142.50	876.26	75,502.60
15		222.00	955.76	92,151.56

7% Interest

Yrs. to Save	Reg. Pmt.	Added Pmt.	Total Pmt.	Int. Saved.
1	$733.76	$7.00	$740.76	$14,779.54
2		14.50	748.26	27,882.56
7		65.00	798.76	95,006.37
10		111.00	844.76	134,267.77
12		152.00	885.76	159,303.67
15		236.00	969.76	245,306.89

12

The First-Day, Planned-Increase
Strategy

This plan is a combination of two previous strategies. It includes the strategy explained in Chapter 5, plus the one in Chapter 8.

Read these two strategies again, and be sure you fully understand them. Now apply them by making one full loan payment on the day you borrow the money. More than one payment can be made at this time if you wish. Next, you must make a planned increase of one percent or more in your monthly payment every year thereafter until the balance of your mortgage is paid in full.

Example

To properly operate this strategy, you must have an amortization schedule. With it you will be able to calculate the number of months which will be eliminated from your mortgage by using the first-day payment strategy.

At the end of this chapter you will find this strategy illustrated using our model thirty-year, $100,000 mortgage at 14.5% interest, with one through five payments made on the first day. I have also shown the planned increase payment from 1% through 10%.

Let's say the planned payment increase you have selected will be one percent per year beginning with the first month. Notice that the entire mortgage will be paid in full in approximately seventeen and a half years, with an interest savings of $218,930.25.

The amortization schedule will be different on each mortgage. To receive your tailor-made schedule for these calculations, see Chapter 15 for details.

Support Information
The First-Day, Planned-Increase Strategy
14.5% Interest Rate

Loan Amount	$100,000.00	Term	30 Years
Pmt.	$1,224.56	Total Interest	$121,909.88

Illustration 1
One First-Day Payment
Payment Increase From One Percent To Ten Percent

Yr.	%	Pmt.	Prin.	Int.	Bal.
(1st Day)		$1,224.56			$98,775.44
1	1%	1,236.80	$505.74	$13,099.08	98,269.70
2	2%	1,261.54	950.89	14,187.56	97,403.39
3	3%	1,299.38	1,583.90	14,008.70	95,734.91
4	4%	1,351.36	2,496.33	13,719.98	93,238.58
5	5%	1,418.93	3,750.28	13,276.84	89,488.29
6	6%	1,504.06	5,424.04	12,624.71	84,064.25
7	7%	1,609.35	7,615.81	11,696.35	76,448.44
8	8%	1,738.09	10,448.44	10,408.70	66,000.00
9	9%	1,894.52	14,075.37	8,658.91	51,924.63
10	10%	2,083.98	18,688.32	6,319.39	33,236.31
11	10%	2,083.98	21,098.93	3,908.78	0.00

Savings With This Strategy:
Interest — $218,930.25   Time — 18 yrs. 6mos.

Support Information
The First-Day, Planned Increase Strategy
14.5% Interest Rate

Loan Amount	$100,000.00	Term	30 Years
Pmt.	$1,224.56	Total Interest	$116,875.48

Illustration 2
Two First-Day Payments
Payment Increase From One Percent To Ten Percent

Yr.	%	Pmt.	Prin.	Int.	Bal.
(1st Day)		$2,449.12			$97,550.88
1	1%	1,236.80	$678.70	$12,926.12	96,872.18
2	2%	1,261.54	1,167.56	13,970.89	95,704.62
3	3%	1,299.38	1,834.15	13,758.45	93,870.46
4	4%	1,351.36	2,785.39	13,430.92	91,085.08
5	5%	1,418.93	4,084.15	12,942.97	87,000.93
6	6%	1,504.06	5,809.67	12,239.08	81,191.25
7	7%	1,609.35	8,061.23	11,250.93	73,130.02
8	8%	1,738.09	10,962.91	9,894.23	62,167.12
9	9%	1,894.52	14,669.60	8,064.68	47,497.51
10	10%	2,083.98	19,374.68	5,633.03	28,122.83
11	10%	2,083.98	22,243.53	2,764.18	0.00

Savings With This Strategy:
Interest — $223,964.65   Time 18 yrs. 9 mos.

Support Information
The First-Day, Planned Increase Strategy
14.5% Interest Rate

Loan Amount	$100,000.00	Term	30 Years
Pmt.	$1,224.56	Total Interest	$112,058.88

Illustration 3
Three First-Day Payments
Payment Increase From One Percent To Ten Percent

Yr.	%	Pmt.	Prin.	Int.	Bal.
(1st day)		$3,673.68			$96,326.32
1	1%	1,236.80	$851.67	$12,753.15	95,474.66
2	2%	1,261.54	1,384.22	13,754.23	94,090.43
3	3%	1,299.38	2,084.41	13,508.19	92,006.02
4.	4%	1,351.36	3,074.44	13,141.87	88,931.58
5	5%	1,418.93	4,418.02	12,609.10	84,513.56
6	6%	1,504.06	6,195.30	11,853.45	78,318.25
7	7%	1,609.35	8,506.64	10,805.52	69,811.61
8	8%	1,738.09	11,477.38	9,379.76	58,334.23
9	9%	1,894.52	15,263.84	7,470.44	43,070.39
10	10%	2,083.98	20,061.04	4,946.67	23,009.35
11	10%	2,083.98	23,171.21	1,836.50	0.00

Savings With This Strategy:
Interest — $228,781.25   Time — 19 yrs..

Support Information
The First-Day, Planned Increase Strategy
14.5% Interest Rate

Loan Amount	$100,000.00	Term	30 Years
Pmt.	$1,224.56	Total Interest	$107,446.86

Illustration 4
Four First-Day Payments
Payment Increase From One Percent To Ten Percent

Yr.	%	Pmt.	Prin.	Int.	Bal.
(1st Day)		$4,898.24			$95,101.76
1	1%	$1,236.80	$1,024.63	$12,580.19	94,077.13
2	2%	$1,261.54	1,600.89	13,537.56	92,476.24
3	3%	$1,299.38	2,334.67	13,257.93	90,141.57
4	4%	$1,351.36	3,363.50	12,852.81	86,778.08
5	5%	$1,418.93	4,751.89	12,275.23	82,026.19
6	6%	$1,504.06	6,580.93	11,467.82	75,445.25
7	7%	$1,609.35	8,952.06	10,360.10	66,493.19
8	8%	$1,738.09	11,991.85	8,865.29	54,501.34
9	9%	$1,894.52	15,858.07	6,876.21	38,643.27
10	10%	$2,083.98	20,747.40	4,260.31	17,895.87
11	10%	$2,083.98	23,894.30	1,113.41	0.00

Savings With This Strategy:
Interest – $233,393.27   Time – 19 yrs. 2 mos.

Support Information
The First-Day, Planned Increase Strategy
14.5% Interest

Loan Amount	$100,000.00	Term	30 Years
Pmt.	$1,224.56	Total Interest	$103,026.14

Illustration 5
Five First-Day Payments
Payment Increase From One Percent To Ten Percent

Yr.	%	Pmt.	Prin.	Int.	Bal.
(1st Day)		$6,122.80			$93,877.20
1	1%	1,236.80	$1,197.59	$12,407.23	92,679.61
2	2%	1,261.54	1,817.56	13,320.89	90,862.06
3	3%	1,299.38	2,584.92	13,007.68	88,277.13
4	4%	1,351.36	3,652.55	12,563.76	84,624.58
5	5%	1,418.93	5,085.75	11,941.37	79,538.82
6	6%	1,504.06	6,966.56	11,082.19	72,572.26
7	7%	1,609.35	9,397.47	9,914.69	63,174.78
8	8%	1,738.09	12,506.32	8,350.82	50,668.45
9	9%	1,894.52	16,452.30	6,281.98	34,216.15
10	10%	2,083.98	21,433.76	3,573.95	12,782.39
11	10%	2,083.98	24,426.13	581.58	0.00

Savings With This Strategy:
Interest — $237,813.99   Time — 19 yrs. 6 mos.

13

The First-Day, Split-Payment Strategy

This strategy is a combination of the first-day strategy in Chapter 5, plus the split-payment strategy in Chapter 6. Please reread both these chapters to understand them thoroughly.

To use these two strategies together, you must pay half payments every fourteen days until your mortgage is paid in full. You must also make one or more payments on the loan on the day you borrow the money or on the day you plan to begin using the strategy. Make as many payments as you can at that time. By doing this, you will begin to operate two of the most powerful debt-reduction strategies together. Notice at the end of this chapter how quickly the example loans pay off.

To totally understand the savings this combination strategy will effect on your own personal loan, you should have an amortization schedule showing this strategy calculated on your particular mortgage. See Chapter 15 for details of how to receive your tailor-made schedule.

Support Information
The First-Day, Split-Payment Strategy
14.5% Interest Rate

Conventional Loan		Strategy Loan
$1,224.56	Pmt. Amt.	$612.28
$340,840.13	Total Int.	$154,387.33
$440,840.13	Int. + Prin.	$254,387.33

Pmt. No.	Pmt. Amt.	Prin.	Int.	Bal.
1	$1,224.56 (1st Day)			$98,775.44
2	612.28	$61.41	$550.86	98,714.03
3	612.28	61.76	550.52	98,652.27
4	612.28	62.10	550.18	98,590.17
5	612.28	62.45	549.83	98,527.72
6	612.28	62.80	549.48	98,464.92
7	612.28	63.15	549.13	98,401.77
8	612.28	63.50	548.78	98,338.28
9	612.28	63.85	548.42	98,274.42
10	612.28	64.21	548.07	98,210.21

Payments 11 through 409 omitted to conserve space
.

410	612.28	593.90	18.37	2,700.89
411	612.28	597.22	15.06	2,103.67
412	612.28	600.55	11.73	1,503.13
413	612.28	603.90	8.38	899.23
414	612.28	607.26	5.01	291.97
415	293.60	291.97	1.63	0.00

Savings With This Strategy:
Interest — $186,451.18   Time — 14 yrs.

Support Information
The First-Day, Split-Payment Strategy
14.5% Interest Rate

Conventional Loan		Strategy Loan
$1,224.56	Pmt. Amt.	$612.28
$340,840.13	Total Int.	$144,004.33
$440,840.13	Int. + Prin.	$244,004.33

Pmt. No.	Pmt. Amt.	Prin.	Int.	Bal.
1	$2,449.24 (1st Day)			$97,550.76
2	612.28	$68.24	$544.03	97,482.52
3	612.28	68.62	543.65	97,413.89
4	612.28	69.01	543.27	97,344.88
5	612.28	69.39	542.88	97,275.49
6	612.28	69.78	542.50	97,205.71
7	612.28	70.17	542.11	97,135.54
8	612.28	70.56	541.72	97,064.98
9	612.28	70.95	541.32	96,994.02
10	612.28	71.35	540.93	96,922.67

Payments 11 through 387 omitted to conserve space.

388	612.28	583.94	28.33	4,496.70
389	612.28	587.20	25.08	3,909.50
390	612.28	590.47	21.80	3,319.02
391	612.28	593.77	18.51	2,725.25
392	612.28	597.08	15.20	2,128.18
393	612.28	600.41	11.87	1,527.77
394	612.28	603.76	8.52	924.01
395	612.28	607.13	5.15	316.88
396	318.65	316.88	1.77	0.00

Savings With This Strategy:
Interest — $196,834.85   Time — 14 yrs. 9 mos.

Support Information
The First-Day, Split-Payment Strategy
14.5% Interest Rate

Conventional Loan		Strategy Loan
$1,224.56	Pmt. Amt.	$612.28
$340,840.13	Total Int.	$134,729.66
$440,840.13	Int. + Prin.	$234,729.66

Pmt. No.	Pmt. Amt.	Prin.	Int.	Bal.
1	$3,673.68 (1st Day)			$96,326.32
2	612.28	$75.07	$537.20	96,251.25
3	612.28	75.49	536.79	96,175.75
4	612.28	75.91	536.36	96,099.84
5	612.28	76.34	535.94	96,023.50
6	612.28	76.76	535.52	95,946.74
7	612.28	77.19	535.09	95,869.55
8	612.28	77.62	534.66	95,791.93
9	612.28	78.05	534.22	95,713.88
10	612.28	78.49	533.79	95,635.39

Payments 11 through 373 omitted to conserve space.

374	612.28	594.26	18.02	2,636.30
375	612.28	597.58	14.70	2,038.72
376	612.28	600.91	11.37	1,437.81
377	612.28	604.26	8.02	833.55
378	612.28	607.63	4.65	225.92
379	227.18	225.92	1.26	0.00

Savings With This Strategy:
Interest — $206,110.48   Time — 15 yrs. 6 mos.

Support Information
The First-Day, Split Payment Strategy
14.5% Interest Rate

Conventional Loan		Strategy Loan
$1,224.56	Pmt. Amt.	$612.28
$340,840.13	Total Int.	$126,368.83
$440,840.13	Int. + Prin.	$226,368.83

Pmt. No.	Pmt. Amt.	Prin.	Int.	Bal.
1	$4,898.24 (1st Day)		.	$95,101.76
2	612.28	$81.90	$530.38	95,019.86
3	612.28	82.36	529.92	94,937.50
4	612.28	82.82	529.46	94,854.68
5	612.28	83.28	529.00	94,771.40
6	612.28	83.75	528.53	94,687.65
7	612.28	84.21	528.07	94,603.44
8	612.28	84.68	527.60	94,518.76
9	612.28	85.15	527.12	94,433.60
10	612.28	85.63	526.65	94,347.98

Payments 11 through 355 omitted to conserve space.

356	612.28	586.56	25.72	4,024.53
357	612.28	589.83	22.44	3,434.70
358	612.28	593.12	19.16	2,841.57
359	612.28	596.43	15.85	2,245.14
360	612.28	599.76	12.52	1,645.38
361	612.28	603.10	9.18	1,042.28
362	612.28	606.47	5.81	435.82
363	438.25	435.82	2.43	0.00

Savings With This Strategy:
Interest — $214,471.30   Time — 16 yrs. 1 mo.

Support Information
The First-Day, Split-Payment Strategy
14.5% Interest Rate

Conventional Loan		Strategy Loan
$1,224.56	Pmt. Amt.	$612.28
$340,840.13	Total Int.	$118,776.20
$440,840.13	Int. + Prin.	$218,776.20

Pmt. No.	Pmt. Amt.	Prin.	Int.	Bal.
1	$6,122.80 (1st Day)			$93,877.20
2	$612.28	$88.73	$523.55	$93,788.47
3	$612.28	$89.23	$523.05	$93,699.24
4	$612.28	$89.72	$522.55	$93,609.52
5	$612.28	$90.22	$522.05	$93,519.29
6	$612.28	$90.73	$521.55	$93,428.56
7	$612.28	$91.23	$521.04	$93,337.33

Payments 8 through 339 omitted to conserve space.

340	612.28	581.37	30.91	4,961.08
341	612.28	584.61	27.67	4,376.46
342	612.28	587.87	24.41	3,788.59
343	612.28	591.15	21.13	3,197.44
344	612.28	594.45	17.83	2,603.00
345	612.28	597.76	14.52	2,005.24
346	612.28	601.09	11.18	1,404.14
347	612.28	604.45	7.83	799.70
348	612.28	607.82	4.46	191.88
349	192.95	191.88	1.07	0.00

Savings With This Strategy:
Interest — $222,063.93   Time — 16 yrs. 7 mos.

14

The Lower Interest Rate Strategy

Interest rates take a roller coaster ride through the years. They go up only to come down again. Because of the tremendous effect that lower interest rates have on the growth of our nation's economy, the government is continuously adjusting them up and down. They tend to raise interest rates when inflation climbs, and lower them when the economy threatens to go into recession.

A Mixed Blessing

This manipulation of the interest rate may benefit the economy, but it is a mixed blessing to the home buyer. During recession when interest rates are lowered, the home buyer enjoys an advantage. However, the person who buys in times of inflation is forced to pay higher interest rates. These rates have gone as high as fifteen or sixteen percent in the not-so-distant past.

When a person is forced to buy a home with such terribly high interest rates, **he should seek relief from them as soon as possible.** When interest rates go down, he should get out of his high-rate loan into a lower rate.

Even One Point Is A Big Savings

The difference that just a one point drop in interest makes on a thirty-year mortgage is **astronomical**. In the full term of our model 14.5%, $100,000 loan, lowering the interest rate by just one percent to 13.5% will save the borrower $28,506. Just a one point drop in interest can save the borrower over 25% of the cost of the original loan. If that same loan can be refinanced at 10.5%, the total savings will be $111,513.73. This four point decrease in interest saves more money than was originally borrowed ($100,000). That amounts to a 111% savings!

Drop The Old Rate, But Keep The Old Payment

Now, I want to show you the strategy that will cause you to pay off your house even faster. Notice that the payment on your **old, high interest loan** will be quite a bit more than the new payment on your **lower-interest loan**. At 14.5% interest, the $100,000 mortgage has a monthly payment of $1,224.56. By lowering the rate to 10.5%, the new payment will only be $914.74 per month.

Don't Give In To Temptation

Oh! How tempting it is to just pay that lower payment and pocket the difference. **Don't even think that thought!** Remember, **you are getting out of debt** by rapidly paying off your mortgage. Just plan to keep making the original high payment ($1,224.56) on the new, lower-interest loan. If you do this, you will pay off the mortgage in less than twelve years. With this added strategy, you will be making regular **pre**payments of $309.84 each month.

On the next pages you will see illustrations of several mortgages which are moved to a lower interest rate using the old, higher payment instead of the new monthly payment.

Support Information
The Lower Interest Rate Strategy
10.5% Interest Rate

Loan Amount	$100,000.00
Term	30 Years
Reg. Pmt.	$914.74
Total Int.	$76,216.54
Int. + Prin.	$176,216.54

14.5% Pymt.	Prin.	Pymt. No.	Int.	Bal.
$1,224.56	$349.56	1	$875.00	$99,650.44
1,224.56	352.62	2	871.94	99,297.82
1,224.56	355.70	3	868.86	98,942.12
1,224.56	358.82	4	865.74	98,583.30
1,224.56	361.96	5	862.60	98,221.34
1,224.56	365.12	6	859.44	97,856.22
1,224.56	368.32	7	856.24	97,487.90
1,224.56	371.54	8	853.02	97,116.36
1,224.56	374.79	9	849.77	96,741.57
1,224.56	378.07	10	846.49	96,363.50
1,224.56	381.38	11	843.18	95,982.12
1,224.56	384.72	12	839.84	95,597.40
Payments 13 through 139 omitted to conserve space.				
1,224.56	1173.37	140	51.19	4,676.95
1,224.56	1183.64	141	40.92	3,493.31
1,224.56	1193.99	142	30.57	2,299.32
1,224.56	1204.44	143	20.12	1,094.88
1,104.46	1,094.88	144	9.58	0.00

Savings With This Strategy:
Interest – $153,088.08   Time – 18 yrs.
Paid With 14.5% Interest Rate Payments

Support Information
The Lower Interest Rate Strategy
10.5% Interest Rate

Loan Amount	$100,000.00
Term	30 Years
Reg. Pmt.	$914.74
Total Int.	$63,702.39
Int. + Prin.	$163,702.39

14.5% Split Pmt.	Prin.	Pmt. No.	Int.	Bal.
$612.28	$208.43	1	$403.85	$99,791.57
612.28	209.28	2	403.00	99,582.29
612.28	210.12	3	402.16	99,372.17
612.28	210.97	4	401.31	99,161.20
612.28	211.82	5	400.46	98,949.38
612.28	212.68	6	399.60	98,736.70
612.28	213.54	7	398.74	98,523.17
612.28	214.40	8	397.88	98,308.77
612.28	215.26	9	397.02	98,093.51
612.28	216.13	10	396.15	97,877.37
612.28	217.01	11	395.27	97,660.37
612.28	217.88	12	394.40	97,442.48
Payments 13 through 261 omitted to conserve space				
612.28	596.77	262	15.51	3,242.95
612.28	599.18	263	13.10	2,643.76
612.28	601.60	264	10.68	2,042.16
612.28	604.03	265	8.25	1,438.13
612.28	606.47	266	5.81	831.66
612.28	608.92	267	3.36	222.73
223.63	222.73	268	0.90	0.00

Savings With This Strategy:
Interest — $165,603.75   Time — 19 yrs. 9 mos.
Paid With 14.5% Interest Rate Split Payments

15

Personalized Amortization Schedule Information

Make Your Own Combination Of Strategies

Many of the preceding strategies can be operated together. Each time another strategy is employed, your payoff is made even faster.

Which strategies fit your own financial situation best? You may wish to seek the advice of your personal financial consultant to help you decide the validity of using the amortization schedules in your particular case. You should then have an amortization schedule drawn which will show you how to properly operate the strategy or strategies you have chosen. Because each mortgage is different, each amortization schedule will be different.

If you wish to receive an amortization schedule with any strategy from the preceding chapters applied to your mortgage, complete the appropriate form. The amount quoted for each amortization schedule covers the cost and contains a charitable contribution to His Image Ministries, a Section 501(C)(3) organization. The cost and amount of your tax deductible donation will be noted on your receipt.

Most amortization schedules are $30.00. Schedules for the strategies in Chapters 9 and 12 are $45.00 each. Any additional strategy you add is only $15.00.

Make your checks payable to H.I.M., Inc. and mail to:
H.I.M., Inc.
P. O. Box 1057
Hurst, TX 76053

You will receive your **personalized** amortization schedules by return mail. Please allow four to six weeks for delivery.

Personalized Amortization Schedule Application For The First-Day Payment Strategy

(Use for Chapter 5 strategy only.)

This form must be thoroughly completed. If an item does not apply to your loan, mark it N/A (not applicable). The amortization schedule will not be made unless you have filled in every blank on this application. **There can be no exceptions.**

The original amount of your loan: $ _____

The current loan balance: $ _____

The interest rate is a fixed rate: _____Yes_____No

The interest rate is: _____ %

The monthly payment. (**Payment only.** No tax, escrow, insurance, etc.) $ _____

The origination date of the loan: _____/_____/_____
Mo Day Yr

The term of the loan (number of years): _____

The first payment date: _____/_____/_____
Mo Day Yr

The loan is a growing balance loan: _____Yes_____No

The loan has a balloon note: _____Yes_____No

   The amount of the balloon: $ _____

   The balloon note is due: _____/_____/_____
Mo Day Yr

The number of years remaining until payoff: _____

Specify how many first-day payments you wish to make: _____

I certify by my signature that the above information represents the amortization schedule I wish to have tailor-made for me.

Signature:_____

Please print:

Name _____

Address _____

City _____ State _____ Zip _____

Please enclose your check or money order for $30.00 made payable to H.I.M., Inc. Your schedule will be sent to you by return mail. Allow four to six weeks for delivery.

Personalized Amortization Schedule Application For The Split-Payment Strategy

(Use for Chapter 6 strategy only.)

This form must be thoroughly completed. If an item does not apply to your loan, mark it N/A (not applicable). The amortization schedule will not be made unless you have filled in every blank on this application. **There can be no exceptions.**

The original amount of your loan:	$ _____
The current loan balance:	$ _____
The interest rate is a fixed rate:	_____Yes_____No
The interest rate is:	_____%
The monthly payment. (**Payment only.** No tax, escrow, insurance, etc.)	$ _____
The origination date of the loan:	____/____/____
	Mo Day Yr
The term of the loan (number of years):	_____
The first payment date:	____/____/____
	Mo Day Yr
The loan is a growing balance loan:	_____Yes_____No
The loan has a balloon note:	_____Yes_____No
The amount of the balloon:	$ _____
The balloon note is due:	____/____/____
	Mo Day Yr
The number of years remaining until payoff:	_____

I certify by my signature that the above information represents the amortization schedule I wish to have tailor-made for me.

Signature:_____

Please print:

Name _____

Address _____

City _____ State _____ Zip _____

Please enclose your check or money order for $30.00 made payable to H.I.M., Inc. Your schedule will be sent to you by return mail. Allow four to six weeks for delivery.

Personalized Amortization Schedule Application For The Specified Principal-Prepayment Strategy

(Use for Chapter 7 strategy only.)

This form must be thoroughly completed. If an item does not apply to your loan, mark it N/A (not applicable). The amortization schedule will not be made unless you have filled in every blank on this application. **There can be no exceptions.**

The original amount of your loan: $ _____

The current loan balance: $ _____

The interest rate is a fixed rate: _____Yes_____No

The interest rate is: _____%

The monthly payment. (**Payment only.** No tax, escrow, insurance, etc.) $ _____

The origination date of the loan: _____/_____/_____
Mo   Day   Yr

The term of the loan (number of years): _____

The first payment date: _____/_____/_____
Mo   Day   Yr

The loan is a growing balance loan: _____Yes_____No

The loan has a balloon note: _____Yes_____No

  The amount of the balloon: $ _____

  The balloon note is due: _____/_____/_____
Mo   Day   Yr

The number of years remaining until payoff: _____

I certify by my signature that the above information represents the amortization schedule I wish to have tailor-made for me.

Signature:_____

Please print:

Name _____

Address _____

City _____ State _____ Zip _____

Please enclose your check or money order for $30.00 made payable to H.I.M., Inc. Your schedule will be sent to you by return mail. Allow four to six weeks for delivery.

Personalized Amortization Schedule Application For The Unspecified Principal-Reduction Strategy
(Use for Chapter 8 strategy only.)

This form must be thoroughly completed. If an item does not apply to your loan, mark it N/A (not applicable). The amortization schedule will not be made unless you have filled in every blank on this application. **There can be no exceptions.**

The original amount of your loan: $_____

The current loan balance: $_____

The interest rate is a fixed rate: _____Yes____No

The interest rate is: _____%

The monthly payment. (**Payment only. No tax, escrow, insurance, etc.**) $_____

The origination date of the loan: _____/____/____
                                                        Mo   Day   Yr

The term of the loan (number of years):   _____

The first payment date: _____/____/____
                                                        Mo   Day   Yr

The loan is a growing balance loan: _____Yes____No

The loan has a balloon note: _____Yes____No

   The amount of the balloon: $_____

   The balloon note is due: _____/____/____
                                                        Mo   Day   Yr

The number of years remaining until payoff: _____

Specify the amount of your additional payment: $_____

Specify how often you wish to make this payment:_____

Check here to order a standard amortization schedule:_____

I certify by my signature that the above information represents the amortization schedule I wish to have tailor-made for me.

Signature:_____

Please print: Name _____

Address _____

City _____ State _____ Zip _____

Please enclose your check or money order for $30.00 made payable to H.I.M., Inc. Your schedule will be sent to you by return mail. Allow four to six weeks for delivery.

Personalized Amortization Schedule Application For The Planned-Increase Payment Strategy

(Use for Chapter 9 strategy only.)

This form must be thoroughly completed. If an item does not apply to your loan, mark it N/A (not applicable). The amortization schedule will not be made unless you have filled in every blank on this application. **There can be no exceptions.**

The original amount of your loan: $ _____

The current loan balance: $ _____

The interest rate is a fixed rate: _____Yes____No

The interest rate is: _____ %

The monthly payment. (**Payment only.** No tax, escrow, insurance, etc.) $ _____

The origination date of the loan: ____ / ____ / ____
Mo   Day   Yr

The term of the loan (number of years): _____

The first payment date: ____ / ____ / ____
Mo   Day   Yr

The loan is a growing balance loan: _____Yes____No

The loan has a balloon note: _____Yes____No

   The amount of the balloon: $ _____

   The balloon note is due: ____ / ____ / ____
Mo   Day   Yr

The number of years remaining until payoff: _____

Specify the percentage of increase you desire: ____% to ____%

I certify by my signature that the above information represents the amortization schedule I wish to have tailor-made for me.

Signature: _____

Please print:

Name _____

Address _____

City _____ State _____ Zip _____

Please enclose your check or money order for $45.00 made payable to H.I.M., Inc. Your schedule will be sent to you by return mail. Allow four to six weeks for delivery.

Personalized Amortization Schedule Application For The Targeted-Date Strategy

(Use for Chapter 11 strategy only.)

This form must be thoroughly completed. If an item does not apply to your loan, mark it N/A (not applicable). The amortization schedule will not be made unless you have filled in every blank on this application. **There can be no exceptions.**

The original amount of your loan: $ _____

The current loan balance: $ _____

The interest rate is a fixed rate: _____Yes____No

The interest rate is: _____%

The monthly payment. (**Payment only**. No tax, escrow, insurance, etc.) $ _____

The origination date of the loan: _____/_____/_____
                                               Mo Day Yr

The term of the loan (number of years): _____

The first payment date: _____/_____/_____
                                         Mo Day Yr

The loan is a growing balance loan: _____Yes____No

The loan has a balloon note: _____Yes____No

   The amount of the balloon: $ _____

   The balloon note is due: _____/_____/_____
                                       Mo Day Yr

The number of years remaining until payoff: _____

Specify the date you would like to target for payoff: ___/___/___

I certify by my signature that the above information represents the amortization schedule I wish to have tailor-made for me.

Signature:_____

Please print:

Name _____

Address _____

City _____ State _____ Zip _____

Please enclose your check or money order for $30.00 made payable to H.I.M., Inc. Your schedule will be sent to you by return mail. Allow four to six weeks for delivery.

Personalized Amortization Schedule Application For The First-Day, Planned-Increase Strategy

(Use for Chapter 12 strategy only.)

This form must be thoroughly completed. If an item does not apply to your loan, mark it N/A (not applicable). The amortization schedule will not be made unless you have filled in every blank on this application. **There can be no exceptions.**

The original amount of your loan: $_____

The current loan balance: $_____

The interest rate is a fixed rate: _____Yes_____No

The interest rate is: _____%

The monthly payment. (**Payment only.** No tax, escrow, insurance, etc.) $_____

The origination date of the loan: _____/_____/_____
                         Mo   Day   Yr

The term of the loan (number of years): _____

The first payment date: _____/_____/_____
                         Mo   Day   Yr

The loan is a growing balance loan: _____Yes_____No

The loan has a balloon note: _____Yes_____No

    The amount of the balloon: $_____

    The balloon note is due: _____/_____/_____
                         Mo   Day   Yr

The number of years remaining until payoff: _____

Specify how many first-day payments you wish to make: _____

Specify the percentage of increase you desire: _____% to _____%

I certify by my signature that the above information represents the amortization schedule I wish to have tailor-made for me.

Signature:_____

Please print:

Name _____

Address _____

City _____ State _____ Zip _____

Please enclose your check or money order for $45.00 made payable to H.I.M., Inc. Your schedule will be sent to you by return mail. Allow four to six weeks for delivery.

Personalized Amortization Schedule Application For
The First-Day, Split-Payment Strategy
(Use for Chapter 13 strategy only.)

This form must be thoroughly completed. If an item does not apply to your loan, mark it N/A (not applicable). The amortization schedule will not be made unless you have filled in every blank on this application. **There can be no exceptions.**

The original amount of your loan:	$ _____
The current loan balance:	$ _____
The interest rate is a fixed rate:	____Yes____No
The interest rate is:	_____%
The monthly payment. (**Payment only.** No tax, escrow, insurance, etc.)	$ _____
The origination date of the loan:	___/___/___ Mo Day Yr
The term of the loan (number of years):	_____
The first payment date:	___/___/___ Mo Day Yr
The loan is a growing balance loan:	____Yes____No
The loan has a balloon note:	____Yes____No
The amount of the balloon:	$ _____
The balloon note is due:	___/___/___ Mo Day Yr
The number of years remaining until payoff:	_____

Specify how many first-day payments you wish to make: _____
I certify by my signature that the above information represents the amortization schedule I wish to have tailor-made for me.

Signature:_____

Please print:

Name _____

Address _____

City _____ State _____ Zip _____

Please enclose your check or money order for $30.00 made payable to H.I.M., Inc. Your schedule will be sent to you by return mail. Allow four to six weeks for delivery.

Personalized Amortization Schedule Application For The Lower Interest Rate Strategy

(Use for Chapter 14 strategy only.)

This form must be thoroughly completed. If an item does not apply to your loan, mark it N/A (not applicable). The amortization schedule will not be made unless you have filled in every blank on this application. **There can be no exceptions.**

The original amount of your loan: $ _____

The current loan balance: $ _____

The interest rate is a fixed rate: _____Yes____No

The interest rate is: _____ %

The monthly payment. (**Payment only.** No tax, escrow, insurance, etc.) $ _____

The origination date of the loan: ____ / ____ / ____
                                  Mo   Day   Yr

The term of the loan (number of years): _____

The first payment date: ____ / ____ / ____
                        Mo   Day   Yr

The loan is a growing balance loan: _____Yes____No

The loan has a balloon note: _____Yes____No

   The amount of the balloon: $ _____

   The balloon note is due: ____ / ____ / ____
                            Mo   Day   Yr

The number of years remaining until payoff: _____

How much interest will I save if I refinance to a ____% mortgage?

How much interest & time will I save with the old payment?_____

I certify by my signature that the above information represents the amortization schedule I wish to have tailor-made for me.

Signature:_____

Please print:

Name _____

Address _____

City _____ State _____ Zip _____

Please enclose your check or money order for $30.00 made payable to H.I.M., Inc. Your schedule will be sent to you by return mail. Allow four to six weeks for delivery.

197

Please keep in mind that any modification you attempt to make to an existing mortgage should be approved by the lender. Your lender is not obligated to do anything he has not expressly agreed to do in the written text of your loan. It is best to make plans before you take out your loan so your special rapid payoff strategy can be incorporated into your loan agreement. However, do not assume that your lender will not agree to modify your payment schedule. **You never know what will happen until you have asked.**

Section IV
Credit Card Strategies

The credit card dilemma of our day is not totally the fault of the borrower. When you realize what has happened in the not-too-distant past, you will better understand why so many are in such credit card trouble today. The only way to understand how this problem has grown so large is to have a knowledge of the recent history of credit cards.

The Personal Loan Interview

Not so long ago borrowers were required to go to the bank for **personal interviews before a loan would be granted.** At this meeting the applicant would be screened to see if he would be able to **afford** the payment the new loan would add to his budget. This seemed to work as a check and balance which kept the majority of the population from borrowing more than they could safely repay.

With the advent of credit cards, a new responsibility was placed on the borrower. It was now **left up to him to decide** whether he was able to afford the purchases he made with them. As the use of credit cards increased, more people began to find themselves in financial problems.

The Trouble Started Slowly

At first this did not cause nearly as much trouble as it does today. In the early years of credit cards, the total balance **always had to be paid in full at the end of each month.** This kept the borrower's total debt at a level previously established between himself and the lender. However, as the credit card era progressed, there was a new dimension added which brought with it a new set of problems.

Minimum Payment

The credit card companies added the flexibility of **a minimum payment on the balance.** With this, two things happened. First, credit card limits were vastly increased. Then installment purchasing without proper credit counseling became commonplace. As credit limits rose from only a few hundred dollars to several thousand, the ever-growing monthly payment became a way of life. This new **expanding payment** had never before been a part of the average person's budget. Now, impulse items of **significant cost** could be purchased **without any payment planning** on the part of the borrower.

Pre-Approved Credit Cards

With this new kind of borrowing came the final blow to the good budgeting habits of the average individual. Loan organizations began to issue credit cards to people without knowing their financial condition. For those with fair credit ratings and substantial incomes, "pre-approved" cards began to appear in the mailbox. Some of these cards came just days before the already over-extended recipient would have to begin missing payments on his other cards.

Borrowing To Make Payments

Today the recipient of these pre-approved cards can borrow against his cash allowance to pay the shortfall of his already overspent paycheck. With this unsound spending, it isn't long until all credit cards are charged to the limit, and bankruptcy becomes the next unavoidable step.

This does not have to happen to you! Read the following chapter carefully. In it you will find some ideas which may substantially lower your credit card debt.

16

Move Your Debt

Moving your consumer debts to the lowest available interest rate is a simple debt-reduction strategy. It can be accomplished in several ways. It works exceptionally well in the area of credit card debt.

Begin by checking with each of the lending institutions which have issued you credit cards. You will want to know which card charges the lowest annual interest fee. When determining which is the lowest, you should also take into consideration any additional fees charged by that lender — costs such as annual fees, individual transaction fees, and so on.

If you still have unused credit available on the card with the lowest interest rate, transfer the debt from your highest-interest-rate credit card to it. Do this with all your cards until you have transferred as much as possible of your credit card debt to the cards with the lowest interest rates.

Extend Your Credit Limit

If you have an exceptionally low-interest-rate card, ask this lender to extend your line of credit to allow trans-

ference of more, or even all your other credit card debt to
it.

I can hear some of you asking, "Do you really think
they will do that for me?" Yes, it is possible that they will
— especially if you promise to cancel all your other credit
cards. Another thing which will help motivate them to
grant your request is if you agree to move all your banking to their bank. One more thing you can offer them as
an incentive is to agree to allow them to make an
automatic monthly payment withdrawal from your checking account to pay off the credit card account.

Please note that many times interest rates are not set
in concrete. Even if the banker tells you certain types of
loans always cost a certain percentage, try to negotiate. If
the lender knows you are comparing his rates with two or
three other institutions, he may lower the rate — especially if he knows your checking and savings accounts will go
to the bank which extends the desired line of credit.
Under the right circumstances, he may even be willing to
reduce the interest rate by a percent or two.

Every Little Bit Helps

At first, it may not seem that this maneuver will make
much difference in your overall credit card debt. But rest
assured, it most certainly will. The reason this strategy
works so well is because **credit card interest rates can differ as much as ten percent per year** from the highest to
the lowest. If you can effect a ten percent interest reduction, it can amount to at least $100 per year savings on

every $1000 you owe. Even the reduction of one or two percentage points is a savings to you.

No-Payment Debt Reduction

Notice that the debt reduction from this strategy takes place **without your spending even one penny.** It is a strategy which the highest-interest-rate lenders probably do not want you to know.

If you apply a few strategies like this one, you will quickly begin to take control of your debt. Even if this does not get you out of debt, at least it lets **you know you have a fighting chance!**

The Key To Rapid Payoff

Once you have successfully moved your credit card debt to the lowest possible interest rate, be sure you do not make the **classic mistake** most people make. **Under no circumstances** must you allow yourself to pay the lower minimum monthly payment which comes with your new, lower-interest-rate credit card debt. **Keep your monthly payment at least as large as it was before you moved your debt.** When you do this, you will find you not only have less total debt to pay because you owe less interest, but you also have a higher principal payment to more rapidly reduce the debt. Continuing to pay the higher payment causes your restructured credit card debt to pay off much faster.

Move Your Debts To A Second Mortgage

There is another way to move your debt to a lower interest rate. You can pay off all your bills by placing a new, second mortgage on your home. Today these loans are more commonly known as **home equity loans.**

If you choose to use this strategy, check with the banks and savings and loan associations in your area about this possibility. Remember, if you decide on this course of action, the new loan must be large enough to totally pay off all your outstanding debts.

Be Sure There Is A Real Interest Savings

Carefully calculate the interest rate you are presently paying on all your debts. In making this calculation, you must take into consideration the length of time remaining before each of your bills will be paid in full. If you have a low-interest-rate loan that pays off in just a few months, it will tend to give you a false picture of the average interest rate of your present bills. For instance, if your total debt has a four-year payoff, the low interest rate of a short, three-month loan will give you a distorted interest picture.

To properly figure the true interest cost on your present bills, calculate the total interest you will pay on them if you continue making payments until they are paid in full. Then compare that figure to the total interest you would have to pay for a home equity loan. If the interest expense on the home equity loan is higher than the interest expense on your present bills, it is probably better not to refinance but to stay with the bills you presently have.

Beware Of Variable Interest Rates

There are primarily two types of interest charged on second mortgages — **fixed** and **variable**. A fixed interest rate is one which cannot be raised by the bank during the term of the loan. This is usually the safest form of loan.

With a variable-interest-rate loan, if interest rates rise in your area, they automatically rise on your loan. If interest rates in your area go down, the rate on your mortgage will also go down. There are usually **caps** put on these variable rate loans. A cap sets a maximum amount the interest rate can be raised or lowered. Many times the cap will also set a limit on how much the rate can go up or down within any given year.

Variable Rates Are Not Always Bad

If a variable-rate second mortgage is all that is available to you, do not give up hope. Under the right circumstances, it can still work for you. For instance, if you are currently paying an average interest rate of eighteen percent on all your bills, a fourteen percent variable rate with a two percent cap might still give you a nice savings. At its worst, the home equity loan could only go up to sixteen percent. Even if it does, that is still two full percentage points lower than you are currently paying. If interest rates go down, your rate could go below fourteen percent.

If it goes down to twelve percent, that would be six percentage points below your old rate.

Don't Get Stuck By The Point

The smaller the difference between the interest cost of the new loan and the interest cost of your present bills, the more important it becomes to understand the total cost of the new loan. Loan origination fees such as points, document stamps, surveys, attorney's fees, etc., are a real cost in every new mortgage. You must carefully consider whether these costs are within reason before you enter into a home equity loan to consolidate your high-interest debts.

Let me encourage you not to let points scare you off. They are a one-time cost charged on a new loan. There can be times when they are well worth paying if the new loan allows you to move your debt to a significantly lower interest rate. Many dollars and years of payments can be automatically saved if the new interest rate is significantly lower than the old one.

Avoid The Credit-Life Trap

Another additional loan cost could be credit life insurance. This is not a benefit to the borrower. Unless you die before the loan is paid in full, it only benefits the lender. Usually there is little or nothing said about this item during the negotiations for the loan. The premium may simply be added to your monthly payment.

If you desire life insurance to pay off your loan in case of your death, you should consider buying a term insurance policy on your own. This can usually be done at a fraction of the cost of credit life. Although your loan officer may want to include this in your note, **it is generally not a requirement.** Leave this clause out of your new loan agreement. If the bank insists you have this coverage as a condition of getting your loan, buy the policy yourself from your own insurance agent or speak with your attorney.

Get The Facts

Be nosey! Ask questions. Do not allow the loan officer to intimidate you. Remember, he is getting paid to answer your questions. Boldly continue to ask until you fully understand the exact cost of your new loan. Always keep orderly, legible notes on each loan proposal you receive from each bank or lending institution.

Watch For Traps

After you have all the figures before you, begin to think of the traps which might be in the best-sounding loan. One of those traps might be that no early payoff is allowed. Maybe there is no cap on the variable rate. It could be that the late payment charges are excessively high. Do not sign until you know exactly what you are signing. Making the right loan is not the responsibility of the lender. It is the responsibility of you, the borrower.

Use The Key To Rapid Payoff

Remember to never take the new home equity loan at the minimum payment allowed by the bank. See to it that your new payment is at least **equal to the total of all the payments on the bills you are paying off.** Even if you have only one more month to pay on one of the bills, add it to the total.

In moving your debt, you have made a giant step toward your rapid debt reduction. **Lower interest means that more of your payment goes to pay off the balance of your debt.**

Section V

Purchasing And Financing An Automobile

This section deals with an item which seems to get more people into financial problems than any other — **the automobile.** By definition, the automobile must be classified as a necessity, especially to those who live in developed nations. However, there is something mysterious about this contraption. A strange thing happens when it is time for one to be purchased. By some unusual process, the automobile that is a necessity almost always **becomes a luxury. This evolution takes place while the purchase is being made.** For a brief moment **the buyer loses control.** Extras are added to the standard model until it becomes **cost-prohibitive to own.**

I have put this strange transformation into the following short sentence: **"Most automobile accidents take place on the car dealer's lot."**

In the **frenzy of buying,** many people will bypass the basic transportation model they need and buy the biggest, most inefficient model the dealer has to offer. The majority of people I have met with unmanageable debt have one thing in common. They have purchased **the wrong automobile** — wrong for their needs, and wrong for their budget. I have found this one factor, more than any other, to be the major contributor to financial failure.

Your Automobile Is A Short-Term Asset

Because of the average automobile's rapid depreciation in value, it cannot be considered a long-term asset. It must therefore be purchased **very carefully.** It must also be paid for in such a way that when it is **worn out,** there will be **adequate funds available to replace it.**

This section primarily teaches two things. First, it teaches **how to select a car** — one which will fit your need as well as your budget. Second, it lays out a strategy which will help keep you from having to **continuously borrow to replace worn-out cars.** The information in the next two chapters has worked well in my life. I hope it will also work for you.

17

The Right Automobile

There comes a time when purchasing an automobile becomes necessary. A good reason is when repair is no longer economical. Safety reasons can also demand replacement. Probably the best reason is when the old car can no longer transport you to and from work **dependably.** A debt-free car which causes you to lose your job will turn out to be **your biggest liability.**

When there is no cash set aside for this purpose, time-payment purchasing becomes as big a necessity as the new car itself.

Avoid A Foolish Purchase

When you **must buy** an automobile on time payments, be very careful **not to** foolishly purchase one **not suitable for your needs.** Keep this foremost in your mind. **Most automobile accidents take place on the car dealer's lot.** This happens each time someone **chooses the wrong car.** The wrong car is the one which draws you into unnecessary debt with options like automatic air, sunroof, excessive gasoline-wasting power, and so on. The automobile industry calls these extras **"the bells and whistles."**

Rules For Purchasing

When you are forced to buy an automobile with time payments, there are some rules you should strictly follow.

Do not use time payments to purchase an automobile which is an **"ego satisfier,"** such as a sports car, convertible, or super-performance model. Now don't misunderstand what I am saying. **There is nothing wrong with having the best**, the most exotic, or the most expensive automobile made. However, an expensive car should be part of your lifestyle only after your faithful stewardship over finances has qualified you for it. You will know when the right time has come. The signal will be when you do not have to purchase that car on the time-payment plan. At that time in your life, there will be **more than enough to pay cash.**

A little known truth about time payments is that they offer the purchaser the opportunity **to pretend he is someone or something he is not.**

Be Sure It Fits Your Needs

Be sure the automobile you purchase **fits your needs.** It must have sufficient room for your entire family to fit comfortably inside. It must have enough doors for them to enter and exit easily. Remember that it must serve you and your family in **all your transportation needs.**

Be very thorough in making your decision. Consider the **daily commute** to and from work. Think about your **trips to the grocer.** Ample trunk space is a must. Transporting the children **to and from school** and other activities must be taken into account. Also keep in mind the trips you will be making **back and forth to church** each week. Your automobile will have to be suitable for **formal appearance**, as well as being **utilitarian.**

No Gas Guzzler

There is another very important factor you must consider when selecting your automobile — **gasoline mileage.** With the global interdependence on imported oil, there is a very real possibility that gasoline **prices could double,** or even triple during the time you own the car. Don't laugh. **It has happened before!** This means no **brute-force engines,** no **four-wheel drives,** no **turbo chargers,** etc.

Warnings About Warranties

Another item of great importance to consider when buying either a new or used car is **the warranty.** When purchasing a new automobile, **always buy the extended coverage available from the manufacturer.** Be careful that this coverage is backed up by the manufacturer and that it will pay the mechanic's bill **at the dealership.** Some policies require you to pay the bill, then send them proof of payment, and they reimburse you. **Not good!** Many times these bills are **rejected,** and you never get your money back.

Warranty companies not belonging to the manufacturer also have **the potential of going into bankruptcy,** leaving you without any coverage when you need it most.

Used-Car Warranties

If you purchase a used automobile, select the right dealer. Most reputable, used-car dealers offer warranties on the automobiles they sell. Be careful that you understand the terms of the protection being offered. You can be greatly disappointed by **deceptive wording** in a maintenance agreement.

When Half Is More Than All

For instance, a warranty that pays all maintenance costs for thirty days is not nearly as valuable as one that pays half of all repairs for a full year. A dealer who covers all repair costs for 30,000 miles or sixty days is not going to be much help either. While 30,000 miles is a very generous distance to warranty your automobile, **the coverage will only stay in force for sixty days.** It will be almost impossible to expend the generous 30,000 miles in such a short period of time. Find a dealer who covers your automobile for **as long a period of time as possible** with the **least direct cost to you.**

Set A Standard For Charges

Be careful with warranties that share the expenses of repair between the purchaser and the dealer. These can be very disappointing unless the prices of the covered repairs are decided by an industry-wide labor estimation book. Also be sure that all parts needed for repairs will be charged at the **dealer's cost** and **not at retail prices.**

Transferrable Warranties

When purchasing a late-model, used car, always ask the dealer if any of the original warranty is still in force. If it is, find out if it is transferable. If so, immediately register your ownership with the manufacturer **by certified mail**, and request a **return receipt.** You must specify in your request that the manufacturer register you as the new beneficiary of any remaining coverage.

Air Conditioning

If you live in an area where summers are hot, do not purchase a car without an air-conditioning system. The extended time people spend in automobiles today makes this a **necessity, not an option,** especially in hot climates.

Demonstrators Or Last Year's Models

One last note in selecting the proper automobile. Ask the dealer if he has any demonstrators or any of last year's models which will suit your needs. These cars usually carry a **substantial price discount.**

If you are purchasing a used car, ask the dealer if he has a personal automobile he plans to sell. Also be sure to ask if his wife's personal automobile is for sale. Many times the dealer and his wife tend to drive the better vehicles from his lot.

Make A List

With these thoughts in mind, sit down and make a list of what you need and can afford in an automobile. Add the unique things about your circumstances which the new vehicle must answer. Resolve that **you will not deviate from your plan.** Remember, the right car is out there. Refuse to make a purchase **until you have found it.**

18

Financing An Automobile

In this chapter I would like to share some money-saving suggestions for financing an automobile. When you must purchase a vehicle on time payments, there are several things which can help pay it off much faster than the standard 48 to 60-month loan allows. Consider all of these suggestions carefully. One or more of them might work for you.

Sell Your Trade-In Yourself

The first rule in any automobile purchase is to always try to sell your present vehicle yourself. You can get as much as 25% more than you will get from the dealer. However, **do not attempt to sell your old car after you have bought the new one.** If you don't sell it yourself before your new car purchase, trade it in for whatever the dealer will give you, even if it isn't the full amount you think your car is worth. On the day you purchase your new car, it is much more important to **lower the amount you have to borrow** than to get the most money for your trade-in.

Early Payoff A Must

When you make financial arrangements to purchase a new automobile, it is important that the lender allows you the **right to prepay the loan.** Do not finance with the automobile manufacturer's credit plan unless they allow you the privilege of periodical early pay-downs of the balance **without penalty.** Using the manufacturer's finance plan is usually not recommended because they tend to be **very inflexible**.

Always Take The Price Discount

Keep in mind that no matter how low the manufacturer's advertised interest rate is, they will usually discount hundreds of dollars off the price of your new car **if you pay them cash.**

Use All Available Cash

Use all your trade-in money and all the dealer incentive money on your down payment. You should also use as much cash as you can to make the down payment as large as possible. Remember, every dollar you **pay down** is a dollar, **plus interest,** that you will not have to **pay back.**

Bank On Good Bank Financing

It is usually best to go to your bank or credit union for your financing. While their interest rate may be a bit higher than the manufacturer's, they tend to be much more flexible. Therefore they will be more eager to tailor-make a loan for you that can be prepaid without penalty or restrictions. Be sure to clearly explain that it is your purpose to pay off your loan **as rapidly as possible. Insist** that your loan allows prepayment. Beware of interest which is not calculated as **simple interest**. Try to avoid interest which is figured by the "rule of 78's." (See Chapter 19.)

The Down-Payment Blitz

As soon as you decide to borrow money to pay for your car, **declare war on the new loan.** Ask your lender if it is possible for you to borrow the entire amount you plan to finance in **two loans.** Tell him the first one will be **a ninety-day, interest-only loan** for the entire amount of the automobile. Put his mind at ease if he questions your ability to pay off the entire amount in that short length of time. Tell him that the first loan (ninety days) is to allow you time for your **"down-payment blitz."** Promise him you will refinance the lower balance into a monthly payment plan at the end of the ninety days.

Now, you may still be asking, "Why in the world would I want a ninety-day, **interest-only loan?"** The reason is simple. This ninety-day period will allow you time to **add as much cash as you can** to your down payment. During this period you should work as much **overtime** as possible and have a **garage sale.** (See Chapter 26.) This is a time to sell all unnecessary assets in order to gather as much cash as possible for the down payment. This can be **a spe-**

cial time when the whole family gets involved in a ninety-day, paydown marathon. Why, if everyone in the family pitches in, you may be able to lower the amount you have to finance by as much as one-third or even one-half.

Pay Down The Note As Quickly As Possible

Any additional down-payment money you earn during this time should be paid to the bank the day you get it in hand. The quicker you repay the ninety-day loan, the lower your overall interest cost will be on that loan. At the end of the ninety days, refinance the remaining balance for the shortest length of time possible.

Please keep in mind that these suggestions are subject to the approval of the manufacturer, your dealer, and the lender. Before this debt-reduction plan will work, you need the cooperation of as many of those who are involved in the purchase as possible.

The Best Car Will Become The Worst

There is something very important about your automobile that you must keep in mind. No matter how good it is, it will eventually wear out. This means you must have a perpetual plan of action to replace your present car. Vehicles tend to wear out or become too expensive to maintain within five or six years. Because of this, you must pay off your present car loan as soon as possible. If you take five years (sixty months) to pay off your automobile, just as the car becomes yours, it will be time to buy another one. If you have not made financial provision for this, **you will have to borrow again to replace it.**

Pay For Your Next Car Before You Buy It

After finishing your down-payment blitz, try not to take more than thirty months to pay off your automobile loan. Eighteen to twenty months is even more desirable. If you borrow for this shorter length of time, there is a strategic move you can make. When you have made your last payment to the bank, **don't stop making the car payments.**

Yes, you heard me correctly. Don't stop making the payment. Now, **I do want you to stop making your payment to the bank.** You should now start making the car payment **to yourself.** Open a savings account. Begin immediately to make the same monthly payment to yourself that you were paying the bank.

Please consider whether or not you wish to save this money in a regular passbook savings account. You might want to open a money-market account. Check the banks and savings and loan institutions in your area and check with your financial advisor. The amount of interest they pay usually varies greatly on these special, higher-interest-rate accounts.

From the day you start making your monthly payment to your own automobile account, you will find that a wonderful, new thing has happened. **Now the bank is**

paying the interest on your next car purchase, instead of you.

How To Turn $280 Into $10,080

Suppose your car payment is $280.00 per month. If your loan is paid off in twenty-four months, you can begin setting aside $280.00, plus the interest the bank pays you each month. If you do this **faithfully**, it will grow into a substantial amount toward paying for the new car you will need about three years later. With this plan, you should have more than enough saved to pay cash for your next automobile.

Please note that, in essence, you are still financing your car on a sixty-month plan. The big difference in this plan and the sixty-month plan of the loan industry is that **you** get all the benefits. On a sixty-month loan with a minimum down payment, you will have to make payments to the bank for **almost forty months** before you can even sell your car for what you still owe on it. However, if you choose to pay off your loan with the plan I have suggested, using the down-payment blitz and only twenty-four months to pay, you now will have a much different result. At the end of forty months, not only will your loan have long since been paid in full, but you will already have accumulated sixteen months of payments toward your next automobile purchase.

$10,080, Plus An Old Car

Using the monthly payment amount of $280.00 and the twenty-four month bank note, instead of being at the break-even point at the end of forty months, you will already have saved $3,160.00 plus its accumulated interest in the bank. If you keep this process up for the remainder of sixty months, you will have saved $10,080.00 plus interest. With the trade-in price of your old car, you should have enough cash to buy a much nicer automobile than the one you trade in.

Next Time, Buy The Best With Cash

At the time you buy this second automobile for cash, if you continue to save the $280.00 car payment each month for the following sixty months, when you decide to buy your third automobile, you will have saved $16,800.00 plus interest. This amount, along with your trade-in, should put you in a position to choose your next car from among America's best.

By using this rapid debt-reduction strategy when buying an automobile, **driving will be much more fun.**

Section VI

Special Information

The chapters in this section of special information seem somewhat unrelated to each other in their content. However, it is their **importance rather than their subject matter** that groups them together. They are of **specific importance** because of the tremendous loss and disappointment you may experience if you make mistakes in these areas.

The chapter on various types of interest is of such importance that I asked *Louis R. F. Preysz, III,* Assistant Professor of Banking and Management at Flagler College in St. Augustine, Florida, to write it. You will find his explanation to be accurate, scholarly, and easily understood. This information can save you money each time you must borrow.

The chapter on pitfalls is also very important. The common saying, "to be forewarned is to be forearmed," is, to my knowledge, nowhere more practically laid out to the reader than in this chapter. Many covered-over, financial land mines are exposed to keep you from falling prey to these traps.

Do not lightly pass over these two chapters, for they will serve you well if you know them well.

19

Various Types Of Bank Loan Interest And Fee Charges

Understanding interest and fees charged on loans should be of interest to you! Banks and other financial institutions that lend money figure interest and other fees in a variety of ways. Choosing the right loan can literally save you hundreds of thousands of dollars on the interest and fees charged.

Financial institutions figure interest in a variety of ways. These ways are:
1. Annual percentage rate
2. Add-on rate
3. Compound interest
4. Simple interest
5. Discount interest

Let's take a look at each of these. I want you to understand what they are, how they are figured, and the types of loans usually associated with each.

Annual Percentage Rate

The annual percentage rate is a rate that is charged to you by a bank on the amount you have borrowed over a one-year period of time. The rate includes simple interest on the principal amount borrowed, plus other fees and charges. This then translates into an annual percentage rate. For example, if you borrowed $2,000 for one year and the interest and other fees totaled $360, the annual percentage rate would be 18%, or 1.5% monthly (1.5% x 12 months = 18%).

As financial institutions can figure interest rates in a variety of ways, **it is important that you always convert their figures into an annual percentage rate** so a comparison can readily be made. Since most financial institutions are computerized, an official from the institution can usually give you comparative rates in a matter of minutes.

Add-On Rate

The add-on rate is another way that some financial institutions figure your interest on an installment loan. However, this method has become less popular due to the 1969 Truth in Lending law which basically requires financial institutions to clearly state all charges on your loan.

If an institution uses the add-on method, it takes your interest charge and principal amount borrowed and combines the two together. You then pay this total amount back to the financial institution over the term of the note, usually in equal monthly installments. The disadvantage of this method of figuring interest is obvious. When calculating the charges, the financial institution "disregards" the fact that you will be reducing your principal balance monthly over the life of the loan. By "disregarding" these payments, a higher interest cost results than if the institution had used the simple interest method.

For example, if the interest payment is 10% add-on, your principal amount is $1,000, and the term is for three years, your total cost would be $1,300 ($1,000 + $300 interest). Your payments would be $36.11 per month. This is calculated as follows:

$1,000 (principal) x .10 (add-on rate) = $100
$100 x 3 (years) = $300 (total interest)
$1,000 + $300 = $1,300 (total loan note)
$1,300 ÷ 36 (months) = $36.11 (per month)

(Note: Per bank conversion charts, a 10% add-on rate per annum equals an 18.5% annual interest rate.)

Notice that in using the annual interest method your interest would be figured each month **only on the remaining principal balance** instead of the total amount of principal under the add-on method.

A general rule of thumb is that with the "add-on" rate, the annual interest rate is nearly double the amount quoted. The annual interest rate does, however, drop somewhat the longer you finance.

For example:

Method	Loan Length	Percent
Add-on	12 months	10
Annual Interest	12 months	18.5
Add-on	24 months	10
Annual Interest	24 months	18.16
Add-on	72 months	10
Annual Interest	72 months	16.96

(Figures courtesy of Barnett Bank of St. Johns County, Florida.)

Keep in mind that just because the add-on interest rate, when converted to the annual percentage rate, drops over a longer term loan, the total dollars on interest paid out always increase! If you are forced to borrow with this method, keep the length of your loan as short as possible. Always remember to have the add-on interest rate converted to its annual percentage rate. This will give you a realistic basis of comparison.

Compound Interest

Another way a financial institution could figure interest on a loan is through compound interest. Compound interest is calculated on the principal as well as on all the interest accumulated to date. It is an extremely expensive way to borrow, as the following example illustrates.

Let's say we borrow $1,000 at 10% for five years, and the interest is compounded annually. The following chart shows the interest you would have to pay using the compound interest method.

Yr	Principal	Rate	Interest	Prin. + Interest
1	$1,000	x .10	= 100	$1,100
2	$1,100	x .10	= 110	$1,210
3	$1,210	x .10	= 121	$1,331
4	$1,331	x .10	= 131.10	$1,462.10
5	$1,462.10	x .10	= 146.21	$1,608.31

As you can see, the principal plus interest for the fifth year is $1,608.31 on a loan of $1,000. Rather than paying 10%, you are actually paying 60.8% interest on this loan ($608.31 divided by $1,000)! This is one of the most expensive ways to borrow money. **It must be avoided at all costs.**

Simple Interest

Simple interest is figured daily by taking the principal amount borrowed times the interest rate charged. This gives you the total interest paid daily. These daily interest rates are then added up over the life of the loan, to give the total interest amount charged.

For example, on a single payment note, let's assume you borrow $1,000 at 10% for six months. In this case, your interest charges would be calculated as follows:

$$\$1,000 \times .10 \times \frac{183 \text{ (days)}}{365 \text{ (days)}} \text{ (or .50)} = \$50$$

Your interest payment, then, for borrowing $1,000 will be $50. At the end of six months, you would pay back to the financial institution $1,050. Using this same example, but extending the length of the loan to one year, you would have a simple interest amount of $100 to pay.

On an installment note, with an annual simple interest rate of 10%, you need to figure out the daily rate, since the outstanding principal amounts will vary, usually monthly. To figure the daily interest rate, divide 10% by 365 days, resulting in .0274%. The daily rate of .0274% would be multiplied by the outstanding loan amount for the daily interest charge. These daily interest charges would then be totaled to give you your total dollar payment of interest based on the number of days borrowed.

Simple interest is the fairest way of calculating charges, since you only pay interest on money borrowed that is outstanding over a particular period of time.

Discount Interest

The discount interest method is yet another way of calculating interest for an installment loan. When this method is used, interest and other fees charged are deducted from the amount borrowed prior to the borrower receiving the original amount of the loan.

For example, let's assume you borrowed $1,000 at 5% for one year. The interest charge is $50 and there are no other loan charges. You will receive $950 from the bank. At the end of the year you will pay $1,000 to the lender, your interest having already been paid.

Rule Of 78's Or Sum-Of-The Digits

The Rule of 78's is used at times when a borrower pays back a loan early. It is a method of figuring interest rebate on a loan. The Rule of 78's is also referred to as the sum-of-the-digits.

The number 78 is determined by adding twelve months (installments) + eleven months + 10 + 9 + 8 + 7 + 6 + 5 + 4 + 3 + 2 + 1 to equal 78, hence, the Rule of 78's or sum-of-the-digits. When using the Rule of 78's method of calculating interest, the financial institution **insures that they will receive most of the interest in the early part of the loan.**

The Rule of 78's is really a misnomer. Actually, the name is appropriate only when referring to a twelve-month loan contract. For example, when this rule is applied to a five-year, or sixty-month contract, it should be called the "Rule of 1830's." You can calculate this by using a formula where "x" equals the number of months of the loan contract.

The formula is: $\frac{X}{2} x (X + 1)$. If you have a five-year loan contract (a sixty-month contract) the formula looks like this:

$\frac{60}{2} x (60 + 1) = 1830$; therefore a contract of sixty months is called the "Rule of 1830's."

However, remember that **regardless of the length of the contract,** the lending industry always refers to this way of figuring interest as the Rule of 78's.

Now let's see the disadvantage to you when this rule is used. Assume you have borrowed $10,000 for an automobile on an installment plan. The original term of the loan is for five years at 10%. If you decide to pay it off in three years, will you only pay three-fifths or 60% of the interest? No, under the Rule of 78's you will pay more than 60%.

Let's see how this is calculated. First, keep in mind that you've paid off the loan in the 36th month. Taking the original sixty months minus 36, there are 24 months left. Using the formula for the rule of 78's:

$$\frac{24}{2 \times (24 + 1)} = 300 \text{ then } \frac{300}{1830} = .1639$$

This figure of .1639 is the factor for the interest rebated to you for paying your loan off in three years instead of in five years. In essence, you paid 100% minus 16%, or 84% of the interest in the first three years, as opposed to the 60% you would expect.

Based on your loan of $10,000 for five years, at 10% interest, you will pay $2,748 in interest under the Rule of 78's. Assuming you pay off your loan after three years, you will be credited with only $440 of unused interest. The financial institution will receive $2,308, or 84% of the interest for the three years that the money was borrowed.

When the rule of 78's is used, it is an expensive proposition if you pay off early. This is because it causes you to pay the majority of the interest cost in the first months of the loan. If you need to borrow, shop around and find an institution that does not have the Rule of 78's in its loan contract.

Even though the simple interest loan and the Rule of 78's are close in total interest paid, remember that the simple interest method provides early payment flexibility that the "top-heavy" Rule of 78's discourages. The Truth in Lending law has curbed the use of many of these methods, so that the vast majority of financial institutions now use simple interest and/or the Rule of 78's as their primary methods of charging interest.

Variable And Fixed Interest Rates

Another facet of interest that should interest you if you want to save yourself money is variable and fixed interest rates. Most loans are either fixed or variable-interest-rate loans. Fixed rates are interest rates that are set by the institution and will not change over the life of the loan. When you have a fixed rate loan, you will not have any increased interest surprises. The monthly payments or single payments will not vary. A fixed payment loan fits nicely into a budget since the amounts do not fluctuate.

On the other hand, a variable-interest-rate loan is generally tied to money market rates, such as the prime rate. The prime rate is the interest rate that a bank charges its very best customer.

For example, if the institution states they will charge you prime plus two and the prime rate is 8%, then your rate will be 10%. If the prime rate drops to 7%, then your rate will drop to 9%. Many of these variable-rate loans will state a floor and ceiling. This means that there is an established minimum and maximum that the institution will charge you no matter how high or low the prime rate goes. With a variable-rate loan your monthly payments could vary from month to month, or year to year, making your budget more difficult to manage. Variable-interest-rate loans are used primarily on mortgage loans because of their long-term nature.

Other Fees And Charges

Remember, interest charges are not necessarily the only charges you pay when borrowing or refinancing. In addition to the interest you have to pay, you also could pay points, origination fees, prepayment penalties, service charges, and other charges and fees, depending on the loan agreement. Let's examine each one of these.

Points: A vague-sounding word, "points" is basically an easy concept to understand. The term is primarily used when discussing a mortgage loan. Some institutions call these "discount points" to distinguish them from origination fees, which also can be quoted in points.

Points, in essence, are an additional finance charge that a lender applies up front, prior to a borrower receiving the proceeds of a loan. One point is 1% of the amount being borrowed. Sometimes fractions of a point are charged. If a financial institution charges you two points, this translates into 2% of the amount of the loan.

For example, let's say you borrowed $80,000 at 10% over 25 years for a home you want to purchase. The financial institution charges you two points for the loan, or 2% of $80,000, resulting in a $1,600 charge you must pay prior to receiving the $80,000.

Origination Fees: The origination fee basically covers administration fees required to "put the loan on the books." These fees are quoted in points or dollar amounts. For many financial institutions, origination fees are points that are set, regardless of the amount borrowed. (Points or discount points will vary with the amount borrowed and the interest rate quoted.) One point or one percent of the amount borrowed is a standard for many financial institutions. Origination fees are used primarily on mortgage loans.

Prepayment Penalty: A prepayment penalty is a charge a financial institution assesses if you should decide to pay off your loan earlier than the original contract states. The penalty will vary from financial institution to financial institution and from state to state.

It is best not to get into a loan agreement that has a prepayment clause in the loan. Your objective is to get the loan paid off as quickly as possible, without being penalized for it.

Doc. Stamps: Doc. stamps are a state tax on the amount you borrow for any loan — automobile, mortgage, unsecured personal note, etc. **Not all states have this tax.** For example, the state of Florida currently requires that doc. stamps be paid at a rate of $1.50 per $1,000 borrowed. If you borrowed $15,000 for an automobile, the doc. stamps assessment would be $22.50.

Intangible Tax: The intangible tax is used for mortgages. Again, **not all states have this tax.** The amount charged will vary from state to state. In Florida, the intangible tax is now figured at .002 per amount borrowed. So on a mortgage of $80,000 your intangible tax would be $160.

Title Policy: This is a fee a title company will charge you for a title search and title insurance. Title searches lay the groundwork for you to obtain legal title to the property, while title insurance protects you against future claims against it. The fees will vary depending on the amount you borrow.

Recording Fees: This is a fee the county charges to record your title to the property in the official public records. The fee is usually based on the number of pages needed for this record. For example, in Florida this fee generally ranges from $15 to $35.

Appraisal Fee: In order to ensure that the money being loaned for a mortgage is backed by sufficient collateral (such as land and building structures), the lending institution will send an appraiser, either independent or one working directly for the institution, to the site for an appraisal of the property.

Service Charges: These are used primarily for consumer loans like automobiles or unsecured notes. This charge is for servicing an installment loan which is more administratively expensive than a single-pay personal note. For example, one bank in Florida charges 2% of the amount borrowed or $50, whichever is less, for its service charge on installment loans.

Other Possible Charges

You could also encounter attorney's fees, surveys, and inspection fees when borrowing on a mortgage note.

Attorney's fees will vary from region to region. The attorney will look at the legality of the loan contract or will, in some cases, write the contract. It is advisable to have an attorney represent you in all major loan agreements and in the sale of houses and land.

Surveys are done for the benefit of the lending institution, title company, and borrower, to ensure the property dimensions are correct.

Inspection fees are associated with a mortgage where a building is being constructed. Generally speaking, there will be four or five inspections during the course of construction. This is done to ensure the lending institution that the structure is being built to specifications agreed upon at the time of the loan.

A credit report on the borrower may also be required. Not all financial institutions charge for this report.

As you can see, in most cases borrowing money costs more than just the interest rate charged. You must keep in mind that the additional charges, points and fees can dramatically increase your annual percentage rate and the amount of money you will have to pay back.

In Closing

The best strategy to save money is to pay cash and avoid interest and fee charges altogether. However, if you have to borrow, compare and select the lowest interest rates and fees available; pay additional amounts directly against the principal whenever you can; and always plan to pay off early.

Keep in mind, the Truth in Lending laws on consumer loans require that lending institutions state clearly the interest rate and fees charged and how they are figured. Do not be intimidated. Ask questions. The law is on your side.

20

Pitfalls You Should Avoid

No matter how dedicated you are to doing only that which is good for your finances, there are a number of things which can hinder the achievement of that goal. I call these things **pitfalls**. Most people only learn to avoid them **after** they have suffered loss because of them.

Learning From The Mistakes Of Others

A wise man once said there are two ways to learn not to make mistakes. One way is to learn **from the mistakes you make.** The other is to **listen to the advice of those who have already made the mistakes you want to avoid.**

On the next few pages, I will give you a word about several pitfalls which should be avoided.

1. Early Payoff Restrictions

There exists an irritating restriction sometimes put in a loan agreement, which is easily overlooked when borrowing. It is a device that keeps the borrower in debt as long as possible. It appears in several forms in loan contracts and usually **is found in the small print.** Its main purpose is to restrict the borrower from paying back a loan before the due date. This wording usually specifies that the borrower will **suffer some kind of penalty** if he attempts early payment.

The reason for this kind of clause in loans is twofold. First, the money stays loaned out as long as possible. Second, some extra money can be earned through the penalty if the borrower pays off the loan early.

The penalty usually requires a percentage of the remaining loan balance to be added to the amount due if the borrower prepays. For example, if your mortgage is **non-assumable,** when you sell your house you must pay it off before the new buyer can purchase it. Suppose a **prepayment penalty** of three percent of the unpaid balance is the **early payment restriction.** If you still owe $60,000 at the time of sale, you will have to pay the lender an extra $1,800 before your loan can be paid in full. This increases your total payoff to $61,800 instead of $60,000.

Read The Small Print

Read your loan papers very carefully, for prepayment clauses can be written in many different ways. No matter how they are written, **they should be avoided if at all possible.** Ask specific questions. **Do not be intimidated.** These clauses can cause you great distress, as well as great cost, if they go undetected. If you discover such a restriction on a loan you wish to prepay, check with a reputable real estate broker, a neutral banker, or your attorney for advice. They should be able to advise you about the law of your state. Many states now restrict the use of this kind of clause. You can also **write to your state banking com-**

missioner. He may be able to help you remove this restriction.

2. Prepaid Interest

There is a form of interest which is figured in such a way that it must all be paid, even if you pay off the loan early. Sometimes it is called "add-on interest." (See Chapter 19.)

This type of interest is pre-calculated; then it is added to your total balance before the monthly payment is established. For example, if you borrow $1,000 and the interest for the term of the note will be $200, that $200 is then added to the principal balance of the loan. That makes your new balance $1,200. If the payoff time is to be two years, the $1,200 is divided into twenty-four equal payments of $50. If this loan is paid in advance, there is no interest refund. The entire interest cost is treated as a part of the balance due on the loan. This type of loan cannot be prepaid with any savings to the borrower. Once again, **check with an expert in the lending industry,** for some states now forbid the use of this questionable practice.

3. Leasing An Automobile

Leasing of every conceivable consumer good has become popular in recent years. The most common lease is for an automobile. This is a definite pitfall to the average person. The attraction of "no down payment" catches the eye, but it isn't long before the pitfalls of the automobile lease are realized.

Everyone knows that all automobile leases are written in such a way that the leasing agency makes money. This means that during the term of the lease, **you are going to provide them with a nice profit.** There are several ways in which the lessor makes money on your lease.

First of all, you, the one who pays all the money, **never own the automobile.** That means **all the equity you build belongs to the leasing agency, not to you.**

Secondly, you usually will not enjoy the benefit of any special discount or bargaining power when the car is obtained from the dealer. Automobiles are usually leased at **full window-sticker price.** However, the leasing agent will shop the dealers and buy from the one who gives him the highest discount off the sticker price. **He gets the discount at the time of purchase, not you.**

There is a third disadvantage in leasing an automobile. Most automobile leases have maximum mileage allowances. For instance, you may select a five-year lease with a 60,000-mile allowance. That means if you drive more than 60,000 miles, **you will have to pay a stiff penalty** for each additional mile. However, if you drive less, you are **usually not given any refund.** Either way, it is the leasing agency which benefits. If you travel less than 60,000 miles, **they will be able to sell your car for more money,** for it will be a **low-mileage used car.** If you travel more than 60,000 miles, **they will make extra money from the penalty you will have to pay them. Either way, you lose.**

Remember, with a lease, **you never own the automobile.** It is only yours to use one month at a time.

This is very different than when you purchase a car. If you get behind on the payments on a car you are buying, there is a period of time called a **grace period** when the lender cannot take it away from you. With a lease, if you cannot make the scheduled payment on time, you **will usually have to immediately turn the car over to the leasing company.** There are very limited ownership rights to the one who leases.

Please consider carefully before you lease an automobile, for you will **pay all the costs and pass up all the benefits.** Except in special tax advantage situations, automobile leasing is usually a pitfall.

4. Passbook Savings

This is the name of the standard savings account that most banks offer their customers. It usually pays the lowest interest of all savings plans. You can deposit and withdraw at will, but your savings will grow at a **snail's pace.** It may even shrink in value because the rate of inflation is often higher than the annual interest rate on passbook accounts.

Your bank has much better savings plans for you to consider. Talk to your banker. Also, check the rate at other banks and savings and loan institutions in your community. Ask your banker about C.D.'s and money market accounts as well as any other high-yield accounts. They usually carry interest rates above the rate of inflation. **Always be sure your savings are insured by one of the federal government's savings and loan insurance agencies.**

5. Door-to-Door Sales

I approach this subject with care, for there are **a few fine companies** which sell their products door-to-door. However, much merchandise offered door-to-door is sold at **a very high markup.** Never buy at the door unless you are given an opportunity to **comparison-shop** the product in a retail or wholesale outlet. Be ready to **say "no" or be prepared to possibly pay too much.** I say again, some door-to-door sales organizations bring you bargains, but **many do not.** Compare prices with your market.

6. Seasonal Recreational Equipment

Recreational equipment usually comes with a very high price tag. While items such as motor homes and boats can be fun, they can also quickly become **financial traps.** It is not uncommon for these seasonal items to have **high monthly payments for as long as ten years.** Keep in mind that when you own these toys, **you will also have expenses that go beyond the monthly payment.** There will be storage and maintenance, plus insurance costs — all of this for something that goes unused most of the year.

It is not good economics to tie yourself to monthly payments on an **ever-depreciating item** such as this. Instead of paying $300 to $600 per month in payments, consider paying $800 once or twice a year to **rent a recreational vehicle.** You can then use the $2,000 to $4,000 you save to **pay off a part of your existing debt** or to put in a savings account earning interest.

Remember to carefully think before you buy anything you won't be able to use year around.

7. Cosigning A Loan

Nothing can be more discouraging than spending three or four years paying off a loan **that someone else has made.** I have never heard a financial planner recommend cosigning a loan for anyone.

Cosigning loans has divided families and split up friendships. It seems to have **disappointed more people than any other type of loan agreement.** When you cosign, you are promising the lender that **if the person with whom you cosign does not pay the loan, you will.**

Think about why the lender is requiring a cosigner. Is it because **he does not think the person with whom you are cosigning will pay the loan?** If he did, would he require your signature on the contract? In effect, is he saying he will **not lend** the money to the person you are cosigning for, **but he is willing to lend it to you?** When you cosign, the money from the loan **doesn't actually go to you,** but the lender may well be **looking to you for repayment.**

Cosigning is so dangerous that even the Bible warns against it.

> **"It is poor judgment to countersign another's note, to become responsible for his debts."**
> **Proverbs 17:18, The Living Bible**

8. Dealer Extras

There are a number of dealer extras that are usually offered with the purchase of a new automobile. These are items and services which are not offered by the manufacturer. The dealer adds them for an additional price.

These options should be very carefully considered before buying them. I am not saying they should not be purchased, but they should be **comparison priced.**

Dealer extras are too numerous to completely list. However, I will attempt to name a few. The dealer may offer special protective coatings to the finish or the under-carriage of the automobile. He may offer special pinstripe, lighting, and trim packages. There may be add-on features such as mobile phones, special C.B. units, theft protection devices. Even premium tires may be offered.

If any of these things interest you, have the dealer bid on them, but also receive several bids from merchants who specialize in the items you desire. Always feel free to ask your dealer if he will include the extras you want for no additional cost if you purchase the automobile that day. Many times you can have some of these things free of charge if you are willing to bargain and immediately make a purchase.

9. Home Mortgage Insurance

This insurance protection sounds very smart when you hear it advertised. However, in most cases you can purchase a term insurance policy that will cover the cost of paying off your home for much less money.

There is another thing which must be kept in mind when considering this type of insurance. Home mortgage insurance becomes less valuable each time you make a payment on your house. The reason for this is that most home mortgage policies only pay for the remaining balance of your mortgage. Remember, this amount goes down each month.

The best way I have found to insure your mortgage is by adding enough value to your life insurance policy to pay off your home in case of your death. (If you are part of a two-income family, do not neglect to insure both wage earners for enough extra to pay off at least two-thirds of your mortgage.)

10. Zero Deductible Insurance

The zero deductible insurance policy is one that provides for full payment on comprehensive or health policies. Your homeowner insurance can be a typical example of this kind of coverage. Many people mistakenly try to buy **a policy that pays all the cost of any damage,** but when you do this, **you raise your premium drastically.**

Stop and think. **What are you actually trying to insure against?** Do you want a policy which covers the loss of a $150 front screen door, or are you trying to protect yourself against a fire which could cost you $30,000 to $100,000 in damages?

Always take a high-dollar deductible policy — one that lets **you be responsible** for the first $500, or even $1,000 in damages. This will cause your insurance company to lower the premium considerably. They do this because they will not have to pay any small claims. If a baseball goes through your window or a storm shutter blows off, it will be your responsibility to pay. If any big damage occurs, it will be their responsibility to pay. Have those who bid on your insurance coverage give you prices on several levels of deductibles — $100, $200, $300, $500, $750, $1,000. **You will be surprised at how much this can save you.**

11. Non-Interest-Bearing Deposits

There are all kinds of deposits you may be asked to make. They can keep your money from earning interest for you. They are deposits you make with utility companies, mortgage escrow accounts, on automobiles, home improvements, and so on.

Always do your best to keep your deposit at **an absolute minimum.** Check with your home loan organization every year to see if you have any surplus accumulating in your escrow account. In any contract calling for a deposit, be sure it states that if the item or service you have purchased is not delivered on or before the designated delivery date, your deposit will begin to earn interest at the money market interest rate of your bank. Also attempt to include a penalty to be paid by the vender for each day after the stated delivery date that your product or service is not delivered.

Press your local utility companies to find out at what point **you have proven yourself a credit-worthy customer.** Some utility companies may reduce or return your deposit after a certain number of months or years of satisfactory payment.

Remember, **every deposit you make is drawing interest for someone. It might as well be you!**

12. Food Freezer Plans

Let me simply state that a food freezer plan may be great for someone. I must also say that I have never met a satisfied customer. If, for some reason, you just do not think you can live without one, be sure the following points are satisfactorily covered.

The freezer must be **competitively priced**. Home freezers are among the least expensive major appliances. However, they are often two to three times more expensive through a freezer plan. Be sure the food plan is **transferable** to the other 49 states. Get a written agreement that you can buy supplemental food **at the same discount price** as you pay for your original food order. You may need extra portions of some items before the original purchase is supposed to be depleted.

With all this said, let me say just three more things. 1. Be careful. 2. Be very careful. 3. Be super careful before you buy a food freezer plan.

13. Lending

Please do not misunderstand what I am about to say. **I am not saying, "Do not lend."** I am saying that you must **be very careful when you do.** Some very discouraging things can happen to those who lend.

Let me begin with the lending of money. If you lend to friends or relatives, be sure the loan **doesn't turn you into enemies.** Never lend any more money to anyone than you are ready to **give** to that person. If you only loan an amount you can afford to give, **you can always forgive the debt without losing your relationship.**

Other than money, never lend anything to anyone that you are not willing to have damaged or destroyed. If you have an item you do not want harmed, **do not lend it!**

14. Setting Fashion Trends
When you decide you must make the latest fashion statement, **you are involving yourself in a very expensive endeavor.** It is much more reasonable to dress a bit more conservatively, because much of what is considered fashionable is only so for a very short time. A $150 dress that is only in style for six months is much more expensive than a $150 dress which is a bit more conservative but remains fashionable for three or more years. If you must set fashion trends, **get ready to pay big money to do so!**

15. Top Of The Line
Many times the top-of-the-line item is **nothing more than the basic model dolled up with some special trim and a few extra features.** When you spend more, be sure you really get more for your money **than a cosmetic job on a cheaper basic unit.** If you pay more, it should be for **quality, time saved, and convenience.**

16. Credit Card Installments
Credit cards play a very important role in today's fast-paced economy. To use a personal example, I travel somewhere almost every day. It would be impossible for me to carry the needed cash with me, so I carry several

credit cards. However, **I also pay off every credit card balance each month.**

Never make the minimum payments. Credit card debt is very expensive since interest rates usually exceed 15% and top out at about 23%. **Almost any kind of loan is cheaper than credit card installments.** Don't get caught in this trap, for it will rob you of a great part of your assets. If you are in this pitfall, **get out as soon as possible.**

17. Uncapped Variable Interest Rates

Variable interest rates are those which are not set at a specific amount. Any variable-interest-rate loan is treacherous, to say the least. But when the interest rate is not capped, it has the potential of destroying the borrower.

The term "capped" means there is a ceiling above which your variable interest rate cannot rise. For example, if you have a variable interest rate with a two point cap, the interest rate on your loan can only climb up two points.

With a cap you have some protection. Let's say you borrow at a time when the going interest rate is eleven percent with a two percent cap. Your loan could go up to thirteen percent, **but it could go no higher.** If your variable loan has no cap, it could rise to twenty percent or higher if the prime rate goes that high.

Always be cautious of borrowing on a variable interest rate, and reject any loan that has no cap.

18. Convenience-Store Grocery Shopping

Some of the best things in life can turn out to be the worst if they are misused. The neighborhood convenience store is a prime example of this. There is nothing more useful to a community than a small, twenty-four hour convenience store. If for any reason you should need an item or two for the household, and the supermarket is closed or too far away to merit a special trip, your neighborhood convenience store is a real blessing.

However, when you begin to buy staples and other everyday items there, **you have turned your blessing into a pitfall.** Convenience-store prices tend to be **higher** than at the supermarket or discount store. They usually sell only **the smallest sizes,** thus not allowing a discount price for volume purchasing. If you are doing all your shopping in this way, you are paying big money for your convenience.

19. Daily Grocery Shopping

Many of today's adults have been brought up never learning how to set up a week's schedule of menus. They run to the store to buy the groceries for every meal. This kind of shopping can cause the family food bill to be **twice, or even three times higher** than it would be if groceries were purchased for an entire week **all at one time.**

Buying groceries daily does not allow you to buy in volume the items you will be using for several meals. That means you will be buying several smaller, and usually more expensive, portions of the same thing. It also keeps you from shopping according to your budget. The daily shopper will tend to shop for **taste** rather than **economy,** and this can be very expensive. If a week's groceries are purchased at once, favorite meals can be planned for special times, and less costly meals can be prepared at other times.

20. No-Grocery-List Shopping
Never go grocery shopping without a well-planned shopping list. If you do, invariably **you will miss buying needed items.** This will force you to make unnecessary trips back to the store, **increasing your gasoline bill.** Not having a list to shop from will also cause **duplication of items you already have** at home but have forgotten about.

Simply write out a menu for each day of the week and carefully list what you need for preparing each meal. Your list should be made thoroughly and as completely as possible. Check the cupboards and refrigerator to be sure you are not putting items on your list which you already have on hand. Also be careful not to duplicate **freezer items,** which can be easily done as frost builds up and obscures labels.

21. Grocery Shopping When Hungry
Never go grocery shopping when you are hungry. This practice will cause you to purchase things you would never buy if you were not **under the pressure of your appetite.** Always shop when you have eaten a full meal. This will allow you to purchase **according to your list and not according to what your stomach craves.**

22. Shopping In Unfamiliar Stores

You will spend extra time looking for what you need and be less aware of price differences in an unfamiliar store. You should get to know the stores in your area. Make your grocery list according to the layout. The time you save can be better spent on other endeavors.

23. Full Fare Airline Tickets

Always try to plan an air trip well in advance. Discount fares are available if you purchase ahead of time. They may be reduced by as much as 80%, depending on how early you book your flight. Tickets purchased at the last minute are usually charged at full price. There is nothing more discouraging than paying $700 for your seat and flying next to someone who paid only $199 because he booked in advance. However, your plans must be firm, for many discounted tickets are non-refundable or a penalty may be charged.

24. Non-Assumption Clauses In Home Loans

Always attempt to see that clauses which prevent a new owner from assuming your present home loan are removed from the agreement before you sign. I realize this is becoming harder and harder to accomplish as most lenders want the right to **qualify new buyers.** They also want the **right to raise the interest rate** for the next buyer. Even if it makes everyone uncomfortable, **press to have the non-assumable clause removed** from your loan agreement, for it may be a hindrance to you when you try to sell your home.

However, also carefully read any clause which does allow assumption of your loan. For example, some assumption clauses may make you the guarantor of the purchaser's payment of the loan. That means if the new buyer does not pay, you may be expected to pay. Your attorney should be consulted before signing any mortgage document.

Section VII

Additional Information

In today's technical society, there are so many things you should know that a section like this one could easily become volumes instead of just a few helpful hints. I have placed these chapters in this book for a specific purpose. Some of the things you might decide to do in order to become debt free **sound simple.** But when you attempt to carry them out, you may find you do not know how to accomplish some of them.

For instance, the chapter written to help you **avoid buying a haunting house** deals with an area that is often ignored. When the average person buys a house, he makes **the largest purchase of his life** without the slightest notion of what he is doing. This chapter will help you avoid foolishly buying a home which will come back to haunt you. Purchasing the wrong home can cause great difficulty to the person who truly desires to be debt free. A home in the **wrong location** can cost you big money. A **structurally unsound** home can put even the most careful person deeper into debt.

The chapter written to help you **quickly sell a house** gives you a twofold benefit. It helps you **get the optimum dollar for your home,** and **sell it in the quickest possible time frame.** These are the two most important aspects of selling anything. These same things hold true when an automobile must be sold. It can take months, or it can take days. **Proper preparation makes the difference.** When you have purchased the wrong house or vehicle, **quickly selling it may be your best rapid debt-reduction strategy.**

I am sure you realize that everything advertised in the classified section does not sell. The truth is that much of what is advertised in the classified section **never sells.** The expense of the ad is often wasted. When you want to sell your surplus to help reduce your debt, the last thing you need is to **spend money on an ad that accomplishes nothing.** This chapter will help you write an effective advertisement.

The chapter on garage sales could well be one of the most important in this book. When you have a sale of surplus goods, you must realize that **many others will be attempting to sell their goods on the same day.** Yes, you heard right. When you decide to sell those things you do not wish to keep, you will be in competition with others in your city who have things to sell. Therefore, **the better informed you are,** the more successful your sale will be. The more successful you are, **the more dollars you will have to apply to your own war on debt!**

21

Don't Buy A Haunting House

The purchase of a home is the largest single investment the average person will ever make. It can be a blessing, or it can be a nightmare. This chapter title says it all. **Don't let this very special purchase become a bad experience.** You must be careful not to buy a home **that will come back to haunt you.**

If your home turns out to be a "money pit," you will never get out of debt. If it is located in an area which causes it to lose value, your rapid debt reduction will not be nearly as rewarding. Because no one wants a haunting house, I have put this special chapter in my book.

Get These Things Right

Location: There is an old real estate salesman's saying that every home buyer should know. There are **three things that must be right** before a piece of property is worth purchasing.

1. The **location** must be **right.**
2. It is important to always buy property in the **right** location.
3. Whatever you do, when you buy, **be sure you buy in the right location.**

Every house can be categorized by its price. There are **inexpensive homes,** as well as **unbelievably expensive ones.** In each price range, you can find homes in **poor, fair, good, or excellent locations.** Even if your present budget only allows you to buy the cheapest of homes, **buy it in the best location possible.**

Try to buy in a subdivision where most houses are **more expensive** than yours. When your house is the least expensive in the subdivision, **the higher priced homes will tend to pull its value up.** Just the opposite will take place if you buy the most expensive house in a subdivision. Your house will tend to pull up the value of the cheaper homes, **while theirs will tend to pull down the value of your home.**

If you have children or are planning a family, be sure your house is located in **a good school district.** Buy a home close to parks and shopping — **but not too close.** There should be several streets of housing between you and the hustle and bustle associated with such conveniences.

Choose your home in a location where the **property tax rate is not excessive.** Do not judge whether taxes are high by the rate in your previous city. Always compare taxes according to the rates in the area where your new home purchase is being made.

If at all possible, choose a subdivision with a **sanitary sewer system.** Also seek out information about what is planned for the future in your area. If such things as a **prison or a sewage treatment plant are scheduled,** pass on that area. It will not be a good purchase.

Termites: Any house worth buying is worth spending the money for **a termite inspection.** There is a three-fold reason for this.

1. It will tell you if the house has termites. If you choose to buy it anyway, as a condition of the purchase, stipulate that the seller exterminates all termites and repairs any damage they have done at **his cost, not yours.**

2. Most buyers **do have** termite inspections performed. At a later date, if you sell the house and did not have the previous termite problem taken care of by the former owner, you will have to pay for the extermination and repair for the person purchasing from you.

3. If there are termites in the home you buy, and they are not detected and eliminated, **they will eventually cost you big money.**

Electrical: The wiring in older homes is usually not adequate for today's modern appliances. There should be a complete inspection and test of all electrical switches, wiring, main power panel, and load capacity made by a licensed electrician. **Ask for a written report** with prices for repairs.

Plumbing: A certified plumber should inspect everything having to do with the plumbing and sewer. **Ask for a written report** with prices for repair.

Heating and Air-conditioning: Both the heating and cooling systems should be checked by a certified heating and air-conditioning specialist. Be sure to have the air flow to all rooms checked. **Ask for a written report** with prices for repair. Also keep in mind that heating and cooling costs can be extreme if you have excessively high ceilings.

__Appliances__: Ask for a guarantee on all appliances including dishwasher, garbage disposal, hot water heater, central vacuum, refrigerator, stove, and any built-ins. If any appliance is missing, for instance a stove or refrigerator, ask the seller to furnish you one at his cost. Don't be timid. The worst he can do is refuse.

You should have written warranty policies on all appliances. If written policies cannot be supplied, ask the seller to leave half the replacement cost for the appliances in an escrow account for six months. If all appliances are still operational at the end of that time, the money can then be released to the seller. If any must be repaired or replaced, the cost of replacement should come out of the escrow account.

__Structural Compliance__: You should ask the local building inspection department to have a building inspector meet you at the prospective house to answer questions and give you information. These are some of the questions he should answer for you. Is the home **built according to code**? Is it **properly insulated**? Are there any **zoning violations** on the house? Are there any **zoning violations in the immediate neighborhood**? Have him explain any **zoning restrictions** that pertain to the area, such as no pets, no trucks allowed on the street, other parking restrictions. You need to know everything you can about the house and neighborhood **before you buy. Have a written report made.**

Radon Gas Test: It has recently been discovered that there is a natural, radioactive gas called radon which seeps up through the ground and gets trapped inside houses. It is considered a **very dangerous gas.** There are properly certified companies which will test your prospective house for the presence of radon gas. **Ask for a written report** by a certified technician, with a price for eliminating the danger.

Garage: The most important thing about the garage is that both your automobiles fit into it comfortably. You need enough room to allow the car doors to be opened. You must also be able to get in and out of the house with packages in hand. **Actually park both cars in the garage to see if they fit properly.**

Have the garage door and the automatic opener checked by a garage-door installation company. **Ask for a written report,** with a price to correct any problems.

Exterior Finishes: Brick is preferable on all exterior walls unless it is cost-prohibitive in your area; then the most practical and commonly used exterior finish should be considered. Vinyl or aluminum is preferred on trim. Exterior finishes of these materials will save you money year after year because they do not have to be painted. If the soffits and overhangs on your prospective house are not covered with aluminum or vinyl material, ask the seller if he will have them covered for you. If he will not, ask him if he will at least pay for half the cost. If he commits to paying any portion of the job, **get it in writing.** Then deduct that cost from the selling price of the house, and **have the job done only after you have received several bids.**

Drainage: Always find out all you can about storm drainage in the prospective subdivision. Ask the seller specifically if the house you are interested in has ever had drainage problems. Also ask several of the neighbors if the area drains well. Run water on the driveway, porches, and sidewalks to be sure it immediately flows **away from the house.** It can become a nightmare if water does not correctly drain off your property. If water flows toward the house, it will be expensive, if not impossible to protect it at flood time.

Soil: Get a report from the local building inspection department as to whether the soil in your area is stable. If it contains bentonite or any other expanding soil, you must be assured that proper construction techniques were used to prevent the expansion of the soil from breaking the foundations. With this type of soil, there is also a real danger that the slab will rise or fall with the wet season. **It is better not to buy** if you cannot be assured that the soil is stable.

Earthquake Faults: These invisible fractures in the earth's surface can be a very real problem. They exist throughout the nation, **even in places where the earth doesn't shake.** Many faults creep and slip, causing tremendous damage to the homes above. Your building inspector should have knowledge of where these silent house-wrecking strata are.

Access: Check the traffic flow to and from the prospective house during rush hours. Notice if there is excessive traffic through the subdivision. Also check whether flooding ever closes roads to and from the area you are considering.

Fireplace: Always build a fire in the fireplace to see if the smoke is being properly drawn out of the house. Be sure the fireplace has a damper which operates correctly. Heating and cooling costs can be expensive if the fireplace damper does not function properly.

You should also have a reputable chimney sweep inspect for creosote buildup and loose fire tiles or brick. Get a written report with estimates for repairs or cleaning.

Cabinets and Closets: Be sure the cupboard space in the kitchen is ample to meet your family's requirements. You must be able to store **all** your dishes, utensils, and other kitchen items. Just because the cupboards seem to meet the needs of the seller, that does not mean they will be adequate for your needs. Take stock of each cabinet and be sure the space is sufficient. Also check the closet space. You should be able to hang your clothes without your garments hitting the back of the closet wall. You also want to be sure the house has enough extra closet or attic space for storage of your seasonal items.

Easements: Have all easements on the property **clearly identified.** Have some small pegs driven about ten feet apart on all easement lines so you can see exactly how much of your yard is dedicated to utilities. An easement could stop you from building onto your house, or could keep you from adding a pool or patio at a later date. It could also cause the inconvenience of equipment being moved across your property from time to time.

Eminent Domain: Through eminent domain, the government has the right to buy your property, **whether or not you wish to sell it.** Be sure there are no future plans for a freeway or other projects across your land. Government agencies often tend to offer less than fair market price when they take over property. Also realize that if a freeway is scheduled to come through the subdivision, or a road is to be widened, property values will usually be drastically reduced, even if your house remains, because of the noise and the undesirability of living next to heavy traffic.

Curbs and Sidewalks: If the curbs and sidewalks adjacent to the home are in poor condition, at some future time your city may decide to repair them. When they do, **you may be billed for the cost.** This is also true if your subdivision has no sidewalks. You may be required to pay the bill when they are added at a later date.

Municipal Services: Check to see that proper services are available. You need to know whether there is **garbage collection** at the curb, or if you are required to haul your own trash off to the dump. This can become very expensive and inconvenient over a long period of time. Also investigate the condition of the local roads in your area. Are they well maintained or full of potholes? If you are a commuter, you need to know about the reliability and easy access to buses or train service in the area.

Roof: Have a reputable roofing contractor or engineer check the condition of the roof. Do not rely on the realtor to do this for you. The roof is one of the most expensive things to replace. If it leaks, severe damage may be done to the structure and contents of the home. Ask the inspector to state the probable number of years the roof will last. Then carefully consider if you will be ready to replace it at that time. If not, have the seller replace it or share this upcoming expense with you. Be sure to get a written report of repair and replacement cost.

Swimming Pool: If the house has a swimming pool, have a certified pool repair company examine the pool and its plumbing, wiring, and motors. **Ask for a written report** of its condition and the cost of necessary repairs.

Crime Report: Check with the local police department about the crime rate in the area. Find out if there is any problem with juvenile delinquency. **These problems almost always grow worse with time.** Avoid a high crime area.

In general, take the time to check every possible thing pertaining to your prospective house. By doing this, you will help guarantee that you do not buy a **haunting house**.

22

How To Rapidly Sell A Home

Sometimes your rapid debt-reduction strategy may call for the sale of your present house so you can move to a home you can afford. In the following pages, you will find some helpful ideas for selling at a reasonable price in the shortest possible time.

Choose The Right Representative

It is usually easier for a realtor to sell your home than for you to sell it on your own. There are certain sales tools available to him which are not available to you. He has access to multiple listing services as well as other advertising methods. The dollars you spend on a **good** realtor's commission will be well worth it if he effects a fast sale at a fair price.

Your Agent Should Know Your Area

Your first priority in choosing the right company to represent you is to find an agency which has successfully sold other homes in your neighborhood. A little investigation will tell you which agents have made the most sales in your area in recent months. Remember, what you want is a "go-getter" who will work **for you.**

The more your agent knows about your particular area, the better. He should be able to tell prospective buyers about schools, churches, shopping, parks, and a number of other things in your community. The realtor **must be sold on your neighborhood** before he can sell it to someone else. He should feel that your house is a good buy for anyone who fits into your price range.

Overpriced Means Overlooked

Remember, today's buyers are looking for a good deal. Your home won't sell **if you are asking too much for it.** Let your agent help you figure out a realistic selling price. This can be done by comparing recent sales in your area. There are dependable, mathematical formulas which will tell you how much your house should sell for. If you have a reputable realtor, you can trust the sale price he suggests.

A Few Dollars Spent Will Bring Big Money

You should be prepared to spend a little money to make your house stand out. It will only cost you three or four hundred dollars to make a real difference in your home's eye appeal. How your house looks from the curb can make a real difference to the buyer.

Touch up the outside paint, especially the trim. Wash the windows, and patch up cracks in the driveway and walkways. Be sure your yard is cleaned up and freshly mowed. Rake up the leaves, and clean leaves and other debris out of the gutter. If you have hedges, be sure they are neatly trimmed. Planting a few flowers along the walkway or around trees, or putting potted flowers on the porch will enhance the outside appearance tremendously.

Cleanliness Says, "Buy Me"

Do a major cleaning on the inside of the house. Your house makes a great impression when the kitchen and bathrooms are spotless. Everything should be put away in its proper place, and if you have unnecessary furnishings, get rid of them. An uncluttered house looks cleaner and **more spacious.** Fill in any cracks in the walls with spackle and repaint. Also, be sure to remove any spots from your carpet.

Put On A Good Show

Keep the following hints in mind when you have an appointment to show your home. **If the weather is hot,** turn on the air-conditioning far enough ahead of time to cool the entire house before the prospective buyer arrives. In cool weather, the temperature inside should be comfortable, but never too hot. Put soothing music on the stereo. A fresh flower arrangement always makes a room seem special, and you can create an inviting aroma by heating cinnamon in a potpourri pot. Put your pets outdoors, and if you have a fenced yard, it is better to send small children outside, too. You don't want the buyer to be distracted or annoyed. Make the house look bright by opening drapes and blinds and by turning on the lights in every room. These few, simple things can make your house feel like home to a prospective buyer.

Be Ready To Deal

Do not let the sale be stopped by an offer to purchase your house at a lower price equal to only a few mortgage payments. Keep in mind that your next payments may be almost all interest. If you let a buyer get away and have to wait three months for another one, **you make the next three mortgage payments.** Only a few dollars of those payments will go toward the paydown of the principal.

When you decide to sell, it should be done as quickly as possible. Selling your home involves some technical aspects, so be sure you have proper professional representation.

23

How To Rapidly Sell A Car

In the process of selling the things you do not need, an automobile may be involved. Because of this, I am writing this section to help you get the most money possible from the sale of your car. Every extra dollar you receive will help pay off your debt.

Prepare Your Car For Sale

Before you put your car on the market, **you must prepare it for sale.** Without a doubt, a car that looks good will sell more quickly and bring a higher price. As long as there is no rust or body work needed, **it should not cost more than a hundred dollars** to get your automobile looking great.

The first step is to **thoroughly clean it from top to tire, inside and out.** A dirty car has very little eye appeal, so a prospective buyer may be turned off before he even hears about how well it runs. This in itself makes it well worth the time and expense involved in **washing and waxing.**

A Clean Motor

Especially important is a clean engine. If you cannot afford to have your engine professionally steam cleaned, you can do it yourself at the jet-spray car wash. (Just be sure to protect electrical parts by completely covering them with plastic wrap.) **A clean engine usually looks almost brand new** and is a good selling point.

A Clean Interior

You can rent a steam cleaner to clean fabric upholstery and carpet on the car's interior. There are also good cleaning solutions for leather or vinyl, and small tears can be repaired with tape or a vinyl repair solution of a matching color. If your vinyl top is showing its age, purchase some vinyl renewal spray to make it look like new. Also, remember to clean out the trunk and glove compartment. Be sure you have thoroughly cleaned all dust and dirt from the dashboard.

Set A Fair Price

At this point, you will be ready to set your price. Remember that **your car will sell quicker if your asking price is fair.** To help you decide what is realistic, compare the following for a car of the same year and model as yours:

1. The price used-car dealers are asking.

2. The price private owners are asking in classified ads.

3. The blue-book value.

You should establish your price in the same range.

You Need Exposure

Once you have set the price, **exposure is the key ingredient.** **Advertise in classified sections** of local newspapers and other publications. (See Chapter 25.) Ads should be short, catchy, and should clearly list your asking price. Also **place notices on bulletin boards** at the office, supermarket, church, or any other place you can. Keep a "For Sale" sign in the window, and **make sure your car is seen.** Drive it around and park it in conspicuous places. Make sure all your friends and relatives know your car is for sale. They can help you by keeping their ears and eyes open for potential buyers. You may even want to **offer a small "finder's fee"** to the person who refers the buyer to you.

Get Your Money

Once you have made the sale, **it is best to receive cash** for your car. If the buyer offers you a check, **go with him to his bank to cash it.** Be prepared to hand him the title as soon as you receive the cash or his check is cashed by his bank.

24

Buying Insurance

No matter what type of insurance you need, there are several things you must consider before you buy. If you will carefully look at the following points, you will be more likely to purchase the coverage which best meets your needs. Remember, **whatever you save in insurance premiums should be used to pay down your debt.**

Consult your financial advisor. He will best know your individual situation and provide you with additional advice on applying the suggestions in this chapter.

1. To the best of your ability, determine exactly **how much insurance you need.** You are throwing your money down the drain when you pay for unnecessary, extra coverage.

2. Always **shop around for the best buy.** Compare different policies and prices. Investigate what both company salespeople and independent agents have to offer.

3. Never let your agent decide what you should buy. He will be able to give you advice, but remember, **he can only offer you the coverage he sells.** That may not be what you need or want. Also, because he is paid primarily on a commission basis, he may tend to sell you more than you really need. Do not hesitate to tell one agent the price

quote you received from another to see if he can give you a better deal.

4. Always **buy the highest deductible you can afford to pay.** The purpose of insurance is to protect you from serious financial loss, not to pay for things you can easily afford yourself. The higher your deductible rate, the lower your premium will be. It is smarter to agree to pay a few small expenses out of your own pocket than to pay unreasonably high premiums.

5. Never buy **a policy you don't understand.** Your policy should be written in **plain language** so you can see exactly what is covered and what is not covered.

6. Whenever possible, **make your premium payments once a year.** In most cases this will cost you less than paying semi-annually, quarterly, or monthly.

7. **Don't be afraid to investigate** a prospective insurance company. Find out if they are licensed to do business in your state. From their financial statement, determine if they are financially sound. Check with friends and other customers to see if the company **promptly pays claims.** Also check if they tend to adjust rates upward after a claim is filed. The agent should be able to give you the names of some customers you can call **for a personal recommendation.**

8. Every time you renew your policy, or at least once a year, **re-evaluate your coverage** to be sure it still meets all your needs.

Homeowner's Insurance

Most homeowner's policies insure your house, property, and personal belongings. They also give you liability coverage in the event someone suffers bodily injury or property damage on your premises. If you own your home, **you should have homeowner's insurance.**

It is generally recommended by the insurance industry that you cover your house for eighty percent of its **replacement value**. Keep in mind, this is not the same as its market value. Replacement value is the dollar amount it would cost you to **rebuild** your home at today's prices. If you allow your insurance coverage to drop below eighty percent of replacement value, the company is not obligated to pay the entire cost of replacement. **They may actually make you responsible for a percentage of the loss.**

To decide the proper amount of coverage for your personal property, you should **make a complete inventory of your belongings** to determine their dollar value. Please realize that, unless otherwise stated, they are only insured for their **cash value, not their replacement value.** In other words, a piece of furniture that cost you $1,000 five years ago may only have a cash value of $200 today due to depreciation. If you want **replacement** coverage for your personal belongings, you must pay more money for it. You must also be sure your policy clearly states that **your belongings will be replaced.**

If you have valuables such as jewelry, furs, or original art, they may not be fully covered under your homeowner's policy. Talk to your agent and determine whether it is worth the extra cost to insure these items separately for their full replacement value.

Once you have determined what dollar amount of insurance you need, **begin to shop for discounts.** Some companies offer discounts for certain safety features such as fire extinguishers, smoke detectors, dead-bolt locks, and burglar alarms. Also, many companies offer a discount if your home is new or nearly new.

Tenant's Insurance

If you rent your home, it is wise to buy **tenant's insurance** to cover your personal property. If you live in a condominium or cooperative, your association fees may already be paying for insurance on a portion of your property. Find out how much coverage the association provides. Then buy only as much additional insurance as you need to make up the difference. Do not leave it to chance. Always be sure your home and personal property are fully covered.

Automobile Insurance

Automobile insurance rates vary greatly from area to area. One of the first things you can do to cut this cost is to **eliminate duplicate coverage.** If you already have a good health insurance policy, find out if your state requires you to purchase additional medical coverage on your automobile insurance. If not, your attorney or financial consultant may advise you to drop the medical portion from your policy. (Keep in mind that if you carry passengers other than those who are covered by your medical policy, you do need to be sure they are properly covered.)

If you have life insurance, there is no need for death benefits on your automobile policy. Also, if you have some form of disability insurance, you probably will not need additional disability or wage loss coverage unless your state requires it.

If you belong to a motor club, towing costs are usually covered, so there is no need to add this coverage to your automobile policy. In fact, even if these costs are not covered in some other way, consider paying them yourself if they are needed. They are generally less expensive when paid on an "as-needed basis" than paying the additional insurance premium.

When you decide how much collision coverage you need, keep in mind the insurer will only reimburse you for your car's **cash value.** This holds true even if you have insured your car for a high dollar amount. Remember, it is the value of your automobile after depreciation that will be covered, so don't buy any more coverage than the replacement cost. Another savings can be realized if you keep in mind that your collision insurance may cover you when you drive a rented car. Check your policy to be sure. If you are covered, you can waive this additional charge from the rental agency.

Shop For Discounts

Once you have determined the amount of automobile insurance you need, remember to shop for discounts. They are offered for a variety of reasons too numerous to list here.

Lock In The Rate

Always have your policy written with a twelve-month rate, even if you are paying your premium every six months. The rates on a six-month policy can be raised twice a year. Unless otherwise stated, the rates on a twelve-month plan cannot be increased during the term of the policy.

Some companies return a dividend to their customers at the end of each year when state-wide claims have remained low. This amounts to a reduction in your premium cost. Be sure you allow some of these companies to bid for your coverage.

Also, be sure to inform your agent immediately if there is any change of status which will lower your rate. For instance, if you move from the city to the country, or if you drop a young driver from your policy, your rates very possibly will be reduced.

Always check the insurance rates of a new automobile before buying it. A good sale price for a fancy sports car is not a good deal if you cannot afford to have it insured.

Life Insurance

Life insurance is designed to protect your dependents from the problems they would suffer should they lose your income. Its purpose should be to provide a way for them to maintain their current lifestyle in your absence. The amount of protection you buy should be based primarily on what your family's needs will be in the foreseeable future.

If there are two wage earners in the family, then both should be insured. A younger couple will usually need more life insurance than senior citizens who no longer have children to support.

To decide just how much life insurance coverage you need, your first step is to calculate your family's current expenses. Now, subtract any expenses which would be eliminated by your death. Also, if your beneficiaries qualify for any social security benefits at your death, deduct this amount. Then deduct any life insurance you may already have through your employer or elsewhere.

You now have a good indicator of how much coverage you need to buy.

The least expensive life insurance is usually group coverage. Also keep in mind that it is more economical to buy one large policy than several smaller ones. For instance, a $100,000 policy is normally less expensive than two $50,000 policies.

The two primary types of life insurance are **term** and **whole life**.

Term Insurance

Term insurance is not a savings or investment plan. It is life insurance and nothing more. Compared to whole life, it is not very expensive in the early years. However, as you grow older, the premiums usually increase. At the same time, the value of the policy may decrease. Most of these policies are only good until you reach a specified age.

Since your insurance needs may decrease as you grow older, term insurance could still be the best buy for you. Most term insurance policies allow you to exchange them for whole life insurance at a later date. This is called **guaranteed insurability.**

Whole Life Insurance

As long as you faithfully pay the premium, a whole life insurance policy covers you for your entire life. This type of policy has the ability to build up a cash value as you grow older. The longer you maintain the policy, the more cash value it gains up to its maturity date. For this reason, many people maintain whole life policies as savings accounts. However, past experience indicates this is not the best way to save money.

Whole life is expensive in the early years, but the premiums do not increase. With certain types of policies, you are only required to pay the premium for a specified number of years, or until you reach a certain age. At that point, the policy is paid in full, and your coverage continues.

Your Policy Can Reduce Your Debt

If you already have a whole life policy, you might be able to use it to reduce your debt. A policy with a high cash value can be cashed out. A portion of the proceeds can be used to buy a less expensive policy, and the balance can be used to pay off some or all of your bills.

Also, many older whole life policies will allow you to borrow against them at a **very low rate of interest**, perhaps as low as five or six percent depending on when they were purchased. If that interest rate is lower than the interest you are paying on your current debts, you may want to use this method to pay your bills. But remember! **Whatever you do, don't leave your family unprotected.** If you cash in a policy, **the protection stops. It is up to you** to be sure you have adequate life insurance coverage at all times.

Health Insurance

In today's high-cost society, it is important to have a good health insurance policy. However, there are so many variables to consider in this type of coverage that it cannot be explained in this book. I advise you to shop around and discuss the many types of health insurance with

several reputable agents to find the policy which best suits
your needs.

25

How To Advertise In The Classified Section

By following a few simple instructions, writing a classified ad can be very easy. Your objective is simply to tell the customer:

1. **What you are selling.** Be specific. Don't make the buyer guess.

2. **Something special about the item.** Tell the buyer why your item is better than the other advertised 25 just like it.

3. **About its condition.** Whether it is almost brand new, excellent, fair, or good, let the buyer know.

4. **The price you are asking.** Most people are shopping for a specific item in a particular price range. They appreciate knowing if your item is within their range before calling to ask questions. **Don't waste their time or yours.** List your price.

5. **A phone number.** Let people call you to ask questions. Then if they sound really interested, give them your address. **Unless you are having a garage sale,** it is not necessary to put your address in the ad.

Your ad may look something like this:

86 Astro Van. Custom interior. New tires. Only 25,000 miles. Excellent Condition. $8000. 777-7777 days, 333-3333 after 6.

You may get some good ideas by reading a few classified ads in your local newspaper and noting the ones that "grab" your attention.

When you place your ad, the representative from the publication you choose will help you with details such as abbreviating common words and how to say the most for the least amount of money. **Don't be afraid to ask for help.**

26

How To Have A Money-Making Garage Sale

A garage sale can be a great way to help pay down your total debt. Don't be afraid. It's not too hard once you know how.

The Best Days

Generally, weekends are the best times for garage sales — Friday, Saturday, or Sunday afternoon. Two-day sales give **twice** the opportunity to make money.

Fridays seem to be the best days because the children are in school, Dad is working, and many moms are free to go treasure hunting. Some people set aside Fridays just for rummaging. Also remember that Friday is payday for most people.

Although many people have other things to do, Saturdays can still be excellent sale days. And for those who work during the week, Saturdays and Sunday afternoons are the only days available.

A few people always have sales in the middle of the week because they feel they have less competition, and everyone who is bargain hunting will be sure to come.

Long holiday weekends are usually not the best times for a sale. Many families make special plans or go out of town. Even those who are driving around during these days are usually going somewhere special. Generally, this is not conducive to a successful sale. However, if you are fortunate enough to live on the main road to the lake or local tourist attraction, you will have a "captive audience" on holidays. Many travelers won't be able to resist stopping to see your wares.

The Best Season

Unless you are fortunate enough to live where it is perpetually spring, the best times of the year seem to be late spring, late summer, or early fall. These are the times when more people are out and about. Cold temperatures or rain do not provide the best setting for a successful sale. Avoid these seasons if at all possible.

Also remember that just before school starts, many mothers are looking for quality, used school clothing.

The Best Time

Most customers can't get to your sale before 8:00 a.m. However, there are many collectors and antique shop buyers who fiercely compete to find the real treasures.

They will usually show up as early as you want to open your sale. Many are up when their newspapers arrive. They read the ads and carefully select the route they can take to hit the most sales in the shortest time. If you open before full daylight, you **must** have excellent lighting on your merchandise, or your customers will soon be on their way.

Generally, most of your customers will have come and gone by mid-afternoon. But if you have nothing else you must do, it can sometimes pay to leave your sale open until around 5:00 p.m. Don't close up too early, for you may get a late customer who will purchase a lot of your "leftovers."

In some communities it is becoming common for working people to hold evening sales in the summer. These sales begin around 6:30 p.m. and continue until 9:00 p.m., or dark. This can bring in a completely different crowd. Those who work during the day, those who are out for a drive, and evening walkers often like to stop and browse.

Advertising

Proper advertising can make the difference in whether or not your sale is successful. Be sure people know what you are offering and how to find you. An advertisement in your local newspaper's "garage sales" column should be brief, but enticing. Be sure to list a few of your most interesting items, your opening time and complete address. Give easy directions if you are a bit "out of the way."

Such items as baby clothes and furnishings, antiques and collectibles, tools or furniture are often sought after and should be mentioned in your ad. Also place your ad in your neighborhood weekly tabloid. These ads are usually very inexpensive but require advance notice, so plan ahead.

A **large sign** with **"Garage Sale"** and your address should be placed at all main intersections leading to your house and also in your front yard. (Check local regulations regarding placement of signs.) Using black paint or waterproof markers, neatly print your sign in letters large enough to be easily read a half block away. If possible, have someone check periodically to be sure your signs are still in place — especially if the day is quite breezy.

Another sign should be placed in your yard indicating "Back Yard" or other directions if entrance to your sale cannot be seen from the street. It is advisable to have some part of your sale **clearly visible** if possible. People hesitate to stop if they do not see an open garage door or a yard full of sale items.

You can also attract attention with helium-filled balloons tied to your signs and strips of colorful banners in your front yard. This gives your sale an **inviting, carnival-like atmosphere**. If you are really ambitious, you can make scarecrow-type signs from two pieces of wood draped with a dress, topped with a hat, and your sale sign stapled to the "arm."

Put your signs up the night before, or in the early morning of your sale day. If you have time and your sale is large, you may wish to put up handbills on bulletin boards at your neighborhood supermarkets, laundromats, or churches. (Be sure to **courteously remove all signs** as soon as your sale ends.) Handbills delivered to the people in your neighborhood will also help stir interest.

Scout The Competition

If you are not a regular garage sale customer, it will pay to spend two or three weekends scouting such events for ideas. At least try to get up early on a Friday or Saturday morning and stop at several sales. You will learn a lot about pricing, display of goods and advertising. Tell everyone you know that you are getting ready to have your own sale, and ask for their experienced advice. Most people love to help by giving you ideas.

Trash Or Treasure — Be Sure You Know

You have heard that "one man's trash is another man's treasure." Be sure what you consider **trash** isn't actually a **treasure** before you sell it too cheaply. A visit to your local flea market should educate you. Those old, chipped enamel kitchen utensils you remember your mom using, and the ugly little Christmas ornaments Grandma had **may be worth a small fortune.** Old baseball cards, comics, Valentine cards, banks, kitchenware, glassware, quilts, vintage clothing and jewelry are often highly sought after. (In fact, if you have a lot of this type of merchandise, including some antique furniture, you might do well to hold a well-advertised **auction.** Collectors and dealers bidding against each other can sometimes raise prices unbelievably high.)

Ready To Get Ready

Now you are ready to get ready for your sale. How do you display your merchandise? **Neatness counts in a big way.** Toys should be clean and all pieces included. Clothing should be clean, ironed and plainly priced and sized. Glassware and kitchenware need to be free of grease and dust. Remember, if you wouldn't want to buy it and clean it up, others will probably feel the same way.

Be sure you have plenty of table space and have all items neatly displayed and legibly priced. Household bric-a-brac, records, books and such should be priced under a dollar. Exceptions include Elvis and other collectible "oldies" record albums and very old collectible books and cookbooks. These may bring considerably more money. Appliances and electronics will bring up to one-third retail value if in good condition. If clothing is currently in style and in excellent condition, you may get up to one-fourth retail value.

Helpful Hints

You should have about thirty dollars in cash in your "bank" at the start of your sale. Most of it should be in one-dollar bills. You should also have about five dollars in change — mostly quarters.

Keep jewelry and smaller valuable collectibles near you in order to be able to carefully watch them. Yes, unfortunately, some people do steal — even at garage sales.

You may want to bring out a pot of coffee or lemonade and cookies. This gives you something to ward off hunger during the sale.

Have plenty of paper and pens handy. If people wish to leave lower bids on certain items, you will be able to let them jot down their phone numbers. If you have a small adding machine with tape, plug it in near your cash box. It will be really handy to accurately total a long list of items. If you are selling any electrical items, have an electrical outlet or extension cord nearby so customers can test them. If you provide a private corner for trying on clothing, be sure to monitor how many garments go in and out. Some people have been known to hide clothing under their outer clothes while in the dressing room.

If your merchandise doesn't seem to be moving as fast as you would like, you can always tack up a "No reasonable offer refused" sign, or "Half Price Sale Today" banner on the second day. You may also want to haggle. If someone offers you $5 for an item marked $10, you can counter with a price of $7.50. You may want to put several miscellaneous items in a **free** box just to get rid of them. It also works wonders if you have a box of toys or trinkets to give small children something to do so their mothers can shop in peace.

Watch Your Cash

Be sure to keep a **close watch** on your cash box at all times, and carry it with you if you must go inside and no one is helping you. If you have a large sale, you really do need a **helper,** especially during the **early rush** of customers. Determine ahead of time if you are willing to accept checks. If so, be sure they are drawn on local banks and the writer has a picture I.D. The phone number should be included on the check, **especially on big-ticket items.**

Figure Your Profit

After the sale is over, don't forget to deduct your starting cash and your advertising costs from your total intake to determine your net profit. **You will probably be pleasantly surprised** at how well you did!

Section VIII

Staying Out Of Debt

This section is probably the most important of the entire book. Many people get out of debt, only to go back in even deeper than before. The following philosophy is written to help keep that from happening to you.

It can help you live the debt-free lifestyle and give you the understanding you need to stay out of the clutches of debt. By following the suggestions you are about to read, you can benefit for the rest of your life.

27

The Philosophy That Can Keep You Debt Free

There is a very important thing you should remember if you want to live the good life, free from the domination of debt. **You must never allow yourself to grow accustomed to living with debt.**

I Am Not Saying, "Never Borrow"

That's right! I am not saying that you should never borrow. There are times when a person might have to borrow. I have already mentioned some of them in this book. The thing that will help keep you debt free **is to never allow yourself to live with any loan for its full term.** Whenever you must borrow, always totally dedicate yourself to paying off the loan **ahead of time.**

Lending Is A Legitimate Industry

Make no mistake about it. The lending industry plays a very important role in our nation's economy. It would be next to impossible for most families to own houses if it were not for the convenience of time payments. Emergencies would rule in our lives if we did not have a lending industry to help meet needs in times of disaster. Even the emergency of an untimely automobile breakdown would be a disaster for some if they could not borrow.

Business loans are many times the only way a small business can get started.

Never Allow A Lifestyle of Debt

What I am saying is that debt should never be allowed to become a **lifestyle.** Always expend all the energy and resources at your disposal to pay off any and all loans as soon as possible.

A Final Word

I do hope that some of the things I have shared with you in this book have helped you. My sincere desire is that you will soon be debt free. You will find it is a much more pleasant activity to budget **for a prosperous future** instead of constantly having to budget payments **for that which you have borrowed in the past.**

God's best to you, and may your life and service to God be enriched by this information.

John Avanzini was born in Paramaribo, Surinam, South America, in 1936. He was raised and educated in Texas, and received his doctorate in philosophy from Baptist Christian University, Shreveport, Louisiana. Dr. Avanzini now resides with his wife, Patricia, in Fort Worth, Texas, where he is the Director of His Image Ministries.

Dr. Avanzini's television program, *Principles of Biblical Economics,* is aired five times per day, seven days per week, by more than 550 television stations from coast to coast. He speaks nationally and internationally in conferences and seminars every week. His ministry is worldwide, and many of his vibrant teachings are now available in tape and book form.

Dr. Avanzini is an extraordinary teacher of the Word of God, bringing forth many of the present truths that God is using in these days to prepare the Body of Christ for His triumphant return.

To contact John Avanzini, write:

John Avanzini
P. O. Box 1057
Hurst, Texas 76053

*Please include your prayer requests and
comments when you write.*

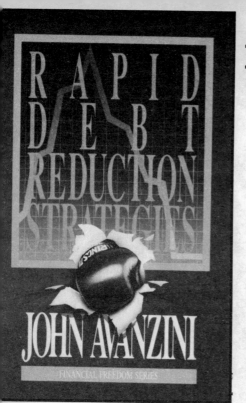

Rapid Debt Reduction Strategies

Learn how to rapidly pay off your debts — your mortgage included!

$12.95

Order form, see page 320

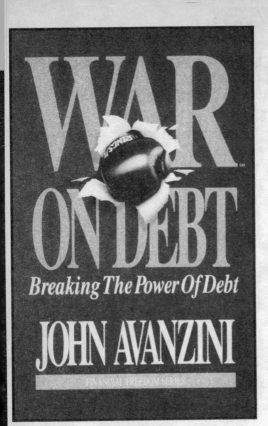

WAR
ON
DEBT

Breaking The Power Of Debt

JOHN AVANZINI

FINANCIAL FREEDOM SERIES

$8.00

Does it look as though you will neve experience financial freedom?

Your situation is not hopeless. God ha a miraculous solution!

In this book, John Avanzini show from Scripture that God does not wan you burdened with the responsibility c debt.

WEALTH TRANSFER SYSTEM

$29.95

This Album contains an outstanding book entitled <u>The Wealth of The World</u> *which deals with the transfer of wealth from the world into the Kingdom of GOD!*

This Album also includes an edited form of the book (with supporting Scriptures) being read to you so you can get these valuable truths into your spirit even while you drive or work!

FOUNDATION PACK

$29.95

The Foundation Pack contains _Powerfu_ _Principles_ _of_ _In_ _crease_, a series of 9(lessons on the prin ciples of biblical pros perity.

This album includes three tapes containing 37 Scriptures on giving, receiving, and God's abur dance that will give you a true picture of how Go(feels about money. This information will help yo break the traditions that have kept you from receiv ing from God!

THE SCHOOL OF BIBLICAL ECONOMICS

Home Edition

$140.00 Worth of Tapes and Books for only $70.00

$70.00

INCLUDED:

* GOD'S WEALTH TRANSFER SYSTEM
- 1 book - <u>The Wealth of the World</u>
  God's proven wealth transfer system.
- 3 tapes - An edited version of this book with supporting Scriptures.

* BUILDING THE FOUNDATIONS OF BIBLICAL ECONOMICS
- 1 book - <u>Powerful Principles of Increase</u>
  Ninety powerful lessons on biblical economics.
- 3 tapes - 377 Scriptures dealing with giving, receiving, and God's abundance.

* THE SCHOOL OF BIBLICAL ECONOMICS TAPES
- 8 tapes - The teachings of John and Patricia Avanzini from an actual School of Biblical Economics.

* STUDY GUIDE
This study guide highlights the books and tapes in this home course to help you better understand God's principles of biblical economics, and how you can put them to work in your life.

FAITH EXTENDERS

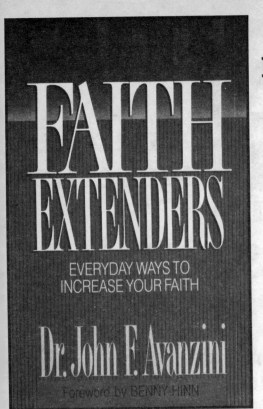

$8.00

GOD IS REACHING OUT TO YOU. IS YOUR FAITH REACHING BACK TO HIM?

Sometimes we are so overwhelmed by our needs and problems that we think even God's power is not big enough to help us. Our faith is often too small to reach out to Him and receive His grace.

In <u>Faith Extenders</u>, John Avanzini distills from the Bible the secrets of how to act in ways that make our faith grow stronger. The men and women we recognize as Bible heroes were human beings just like us. They suffered, they had problems, they failed, and they sinned. Then what made them heroes? It was their ability to focus on situations, events, people and simple things as ways of magnifying their faith. <u>Faith Extenders</u> teaches us how to respond to our daily circumstances in a manner that increases our faith and helps us to tap into the power God wants us to have.

STOLEN PROPERTY RETURNED

$6.00

When You Have Been "Ripped Off," "Robbed" and "Stolen From," Where Can You Go for Help?

There Is an Answer in the Bible That Always Gets Results!

Every one of us has had something of value stolen from him. It may have been in business, a family relationship, a wayward child, a promotion on the job, or even large sums of money. In the midst of these terrible assaults we seem powerless to recover our losses.

John Avanzini reveals to us, in Stolen Property Returned, *how to take the thief into the heavenly courtroom, where God is the judge and Jesus is the prosecuting attorney. In this courtroom the verdict is guaranteed in our favor.*

Based on principles he has seen proven in his own life, Dr. Avanzini provides you with the laws of harvest, God's plan for you to live abundantly!

$8.00

30 60
HUNDREDFOLD

You will learn:

How to determine whether you are planting in good or bad soil.

The importance of replanting part of your harvest.

How to maintain the "crops" until harvest.

The importance of giving and the benefits God has for faithful givers.

How to apply the laws of harvest and use the principles God has established.

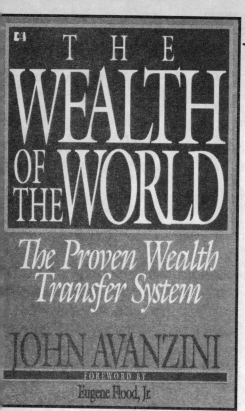

$7.00

THE WEALTH OF THE WORLD

The Wealth of the World answers the following questions and others with balanced, biblical teaching that will change your thinking about money and will open the doors for you to walk in overflowing abundance.

Is it true? Does the wealth of the sinner really belong to the just, the righteous of God?

Is it really God's desire to see all of His children blessed?

What purpose would God have in blessing His children to such an extent?

Order form, see page 320

POWERFUL PRINCIPLES *of* INCREASE

Are you tired of being continuously short of the finances you need to fully and completely obey God?

Would you like to begin to operate in a bold new cycle of abundance with God?

Do you want to have a part in financing the great end-time harvest?

$9.00

Powerful <u>Principles</u> <u>of</u> <u>Increase</u> is a series of lessons designed to help you experience the financial breakthrough you have been desiring. Some of the lessons include:

> How You Can Reap in a Recession
> 10 Truths About Money
> Five Major Mistakes About Money
> The Abundance of God
> God—The Greatest Giver
> Five Kinds of Giving

Learn how you can experience God's abundance and be a blessing to others.

In this exciting book by John Avanzini, we have key after key spelled out from the Word of God showing us we can take the resources of this world and use them to establish God's Kingdom! Let's read them and then do them in Jesus' name!
PAUL F. CROUCH
Trinity Broadcasting Network, Inc.

ORDER FORM

NAME _____

ADDRESS_____

CITY_____ STATE_____ ZIP_____ PHONE _____

☐VISA ☐MASTERCARD ☐CHECK

CREDIT CARD # _____ EXP. DATE_____

DESCRIPTION	UNIT COUNT	UNIT PRICE	AMOUNT
30/60/Hundredfold		$8.00	
Always Abounding		$6.00	
Faith Extenders		$8.00	
Powerful Principles of Increase		$9.00	
Stolen Property Returned		$6.00	
Wealth of the World		$7.00	
The School of Biblical Economics		$70.00	
Wealth Transfer System		$29.95	
Foundation Pack		$29.95	
Rapid Debt Reduction Strategies		$12.95	
War on Debt		$8.00	
		TOTAL AMOUNT	

These books can be purchased from your local bookstores, or by writing:

HIS PUBLISHING CO.
P.O. Box 1096
Hurst, Texas 76053
(817) 485-5997
For orders, call: 1-800-962-8337